TWELVE KEYS TO AN EFFECTIVE CHURCH

Other Books by Kennon L. Callahan

Building for Effective Mission
Dynamic Worship
Effective Church Finances
Effective Church Leadership
Giving and Stewardship in an Effective Church
Preaching Grace
Small, Strong Congregations
The Future That Has Come
Twelve Keys for Living
Twelve Keys to an Effective Church
Twelve Keys to an Effective Church: The Leaders' Guide
Twelve Keys to an Effective Church: The Planning Workbook
Twelve Keys to an Effective Church: The Study Guide
Visiting in an Age of Mission

TWELVE KEYS
TO AN
EFFECTIVE CHURCH

Strategic Planning for Mission

KENNON L. CALLAHAN

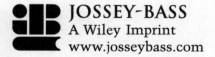

JOSSEY-BASS
A Wiley Imprint
www.josseybass.com

Published by Jossey-Bass
A Wiley Imprint
989 Market Street, San Francisco, CA 94103-1741   www.josseybass.com

FIRST JOSSEY-BASS EDITION PUBLISHED IN 1997. THIS BOOK WAS ORIGINALLY PUBLISHED BY HARPER & ROW.

Jossey-Bass books and products are available through most bookstores. To contact Jossey-Bass directly call our Customer Care Department within the U.S. at (800) 956-7739, outside the U.S. at (317) 572-3986 or fax (317) 572-4002.

Jossey-Bass also publishes its books in a variety of electronic formats. Some content that appears in print may not be available in electronic books.

Library of Congress Cataloging-in-Publication Data

Callahan, Kennon L.
    Twelve keys to an effective church / Kennon L. Callahan. — 1st ed.
        p.   cm.
    Originally published: San Francisco : Harper & Row, c1983–c1990.
        Contents: [1] Strategic planning for mission — [2] The leaders' guide — [3] The planning workbook. New rev. ed.
        ISBN 0–7879–3871–8 (v. 1 : alk. paper). — ISBN 0–7879–3870–X (v. 2 : alk. paper). — ISBN 0–7879–3873–4 (v. 3 : alk. paper)
        1. Church growth—Planning.   2. Strategic planning.   3. Church management.   I. Title.
BV652.25.C34 1997
254'.5—DC21   97–24760

Printed in the United States of America
FIRST EDITION
HB Printing   10 9 8

To Julie McCoy Callahan

Her life and love have enriched our living. Her contributions have been invaluable in the development of this work. Her insights have added richly to the perspective here shared with the reader.

Contents

Figures

Preface

This book is designed to assist local churches in their strategic long-range planning to be effective churches in mission.

During the past twenty-three years, I have had the opportunity to serve as long-range planning consultant with more than seven hundred and fifty churches across the country. I am deeply grateful to these churches, their members, and their pastors for the rich insights and helpful experiences that they have contributed to my understanding of effective, successful long-range planning.

Further, I want to acknowledge my strong appreciation of the following persons for their contributions to my thinking and conclusions about long-range planning: Dr. Thomas J. Shipp, for many years the senior pastor of Lovers Lane United Methodist Church in Dallas, Texas; Dr. Marvin T. Judy, professor, Perkins School of Theology; Mr. Earl K. Callahan, a wise and thoughtful planner; Lyle E. Schaller, with the Yokefellow Institute; and Dr. Earl D. C. Brewer, professor, Candler School of Theology. Though they have made decisive contributions to my perspective, final responsibility for this material and its implications for effective churches rests with me.

Suggestions and new ideas are invited as readers have the opportunity to study and use this book.

In these times, it is important and urgent that congregations build on their foundational strengths as they move forward in mission. It is my hope that local congregations will plan their mission with strong vision and decisive action. A study of these *Twelve Keys* will help a congregation to do this by using effective long-range planning.

Introduction, Part I:
Planning and Hope

Twelve characteristics can be identified that contribute to a church's being effective and successful. In the years to come, it is important that churches put these twelve characteristics well in place. Those churches that do so with a long-range plan are most likely to be effective in mission and successful in outreach.

This book has two central objectives: first, to deliver a general understanding of strategic long-range planning; second, to deliver an understanding of each of the twelve keys to an effective church. The first objective is accomplished in the Introduction and throughout the book; the second, in specific discussions of each of the twelve keys in Chapters 1 through 12 and in the Conclusion.

Effective long-range planning will help a local congregation to achieve mission and success. It includes three important dynamics that enable a church to move forward:

1. Effective long-range planning is diagnostic in its focus.
2. Effective long-range planning is strategic in its decisions. Discussion and study are the modest prelude to major decisions.
3. Effective long-range planning is hopeful—responsibly and courageously.

God's promise draws us toward our future with compassion and certainty. The diagnostic, strategic, and responsibly hopeful dynamics of the approach here to long-range planning make it most effective in helping local congregations to move decisively forward.

Long-Range Planning Is Diagnostic

In the coming years of this decade, local churches would do well to implement a diagnostic approach to long-range planning. A diagnostic approach concentrates on several central characteristics in the local church and its regional community that are considered critical to substantial, solid planning for mission.

Regrettably, too many churches have employed a data-collection approach. This approach has been built on the implicit premise that the more data collected, the more they will tell us the direction we should head in as a local church. The difficulty often is that the more data a local congregation collects, the more confused it becomes—precisely because it has not developed a perspective based on central considerations with which to interpret this massive array of data.

Further, the data-collection approach tends to enslave local churches to the alleged inevitability of demographic trends of population growth or decline. Indeed, local churches—confused by the data mass—tend to select a particular demographic trend so as to eliminate, in a simplistic, quick-closure manner, the confusion that the data-collection approach to planning creates. For example, some congregations have justified a decision to withdraw from active mission in certain areas of their communities on the basis of the simplistic selection of a projection of population decline for those areas.

To be sure, there is a modest correlation between demographic trends, church growth, and mission. But there is no one-to-one correlation. Some churches grow in the midst of a declining population. Some churches decline in the midst of a growing, unchurched population. Some churches engaged in substantial mission tend to grow; some do not. Some declining churches are in mission responsibly; some are simply declining—frequently using their reputed mission as an excuse for their decline.

A diagnostic approach to planning provides a local church with a more thoughtful assessment of (1) the central characteristics of substantial missional churches, and (2) the decisive dynamics in its regional community. Both the central characteristics that are found in successful missional churches and the community dynamics are decisive in planning for mission.

As mentioned in the Preface, during these past twenty-three years, I have had the privilege of serving as the long-range planning consultant with over seven hundred and fifty churches across the country. I have also become acquainted with the work of several thousand other churches in a wide range of denominations. Over these years of research and consultation, twelve factors have emerged persistently as the central characteristics of successful missional churches. These twelve fall into two categories: six are *relational* characteristics and six are *functional* characteristics. Generally speaking, effective, successful churches have nine of these twelve central characteristics. Moreover, the majority of the nine are relational rather than functional. Tragically, too many churches have concentrated on the functional rather than the relational factors that contribute to mission and success.

The relational characteristics that a diagnostic approach takes seriously are:

1. *Specific, Concrete Missional Objectives*.   The missional church has two or three such objectives that involve strong groupings of the congregation in mission with persons who have specific human hurts and hopes.

2. *Pastoral and Lay Visitation.* Though a lost art in many churches, the missional church does consequential visitation with the unchurched, newcomers, constituents, and members on a weekly basis.

3. *Corporate, Dynamic Worship.* The weekly services are holistic in music and message, corporately planned, and led by a compassionate, competent team of laity and pastor.

4. *Significant Relational Groups.* Most people come to a local church looking for community. Instead, we put them on a committee. Missional churches are constantly and intentionally starting new caring groups in which people may discover roots, place, and belonging.

5. *Strong Leadership Resources.* Many churches train leaders to fill functional slots inside the church's program. Missional churches nurture a majority of their leaders to be relational and caring with individuals and groups in the regional community.

6. *Streamlined Structure and Solid, Participatory Decision Making.* Missional churches plan on the basis of their strengths, hopes, and objectives. They are less preoccupied with their own needs and problems than many churches. They have a streamlined organizational structure.

The functional characteristics that a diagnostic approach takes seriously are:

7. *Several Competent Programs and Activities.* Missional churches know people attract people more than programs do. Generally, they have two to three really competent programs that serve, rather than use, people.

8. *Open Accessibility.* A physical location that is accessible in terms of major traffic patterns and average trip time and leaders who are accessible to the community are both important.

9. *High Visibility.* Successful missional churches have a high degree of geographical and grapevine visibility with churched and unchurched persons in the community.

10. *Adequate Parking, Land, and Landscaping.* As a national average one parking space permits 1.75 persons to participate in the church. Occasionally, it may be as high as 2.5 persons per parking space.

11. *Adequate Space and Facilities.* More churches underbuild than overbuild, and they thereby limit their growth. They build fixed rather than flexible structures. Missional churches build for the future, with a clear perspective that this is the eleventh, not the first, most important characteristic. Increasingly, they take energy and debt interest issues seriously.

12. *Solid Financial Resources.* Missional churches know people give money to people more than to programs, purposes, or paper. Missional churches tend to put their money into people rather than property. They exercise responsible, courageous stewardship.

It is important to note briefly three fundamental principles about these twelve characteristics of effective, successful congregations.

1. The relational characteristics are the sources of satisfaction in a congregation.
2. The functional characteristics, if they are not in place, are the sources of *dis*satisfaction in a congregation.
3. There is no direct correlation between the two.

That is to say, the central relational characteristics are the key sources of satisfaction and well-being in a given congregation; the more these relational characteristics are present, the higher the level of satisfaction. Likewise, the more the functional characteristics are present, the lower the level of *dis*satisfaction in a congregation. Moreover, there is no direct correlation between the levels of satisfaction and of dissatisfaction related to the relational and functional characteristics present within a congregation: To lower the level of dissatisfaction does not raise the level of satisfaction. To raise the level of satisfaction does not lower the level of dissatisfaction.

The only correlation—if one exists—is that the level of satisfaction needs to be higher than the level of dissatisfaction in order for the congregation to have a sense of confidence and competence about its mission. Congregations in which the level of satisfaction is higher than the level of dissatisfaction generally have a stronger sense of intentionality and well-being about their life in mission; they possess a sense of their own strength and a responsible hope that they can accomplish the mission to which God calls them.

Regrettably, numerous pastors across the country have focused their ministry on lowering the level of *dis*satisfaction in the church they are serving. By and large, they have done this for four basic reasons:

1. Many pastors are supportive, giving, and caring persons who are, therefore, much more attuned to the level of *dis*satisfaction around them than the level of satisfaction.

2. Many of these pastors have been trained in an insidious action-reflection, responsive approach to ministry. Hence, they react to signals of dissatisfaction rather than acting with strategic long-range planning to raise the level of satisfaction.

3. They are also often prone to "quick closure." That is, they move to relieve dissatisfaction and low-level pain quickly because this way of acting has been instilled in them more than ways of working long term to improve the well-being and satisfaction within a congregation.

4. For many pastors, their commitment and guilt dynamics influence them to work harder, not smarter. They therefore preoccupy themselves

with the symptoms of dissatisfaction rather than thoughtfully planning and moving forward to put in place strong sources of satisfaction.

Some pastors are asked to move from one church to another—even though they have worked hard at lowering the level of dissatisfaction in a congregation. This is because they have not worked at raising at the level of satisfaction. Frequently, pastors who have worked hard to build adequate space and facilities find themselves moving the year after the successful completion of the building program. Further, they frequently do not understand why they have been asked to move. Basically, all they have accomplished by putting in the new space and facilities is to lower the level of dissatisfaction about inadequate space and facilities. But the preoccupation with that particular functional characteristic has frequently caused them to neglect some of the central relational characteristics, for example, pastoral visitation or the development of significant relational groups.

The analysis here is more complex than some simplistic hierarchy of needs. Rather, it calls for understanding two major dynamics, satisfaction and dissatisfaction, operative in individuals and groups and, hence, in local congregations. It calls for the perception to see the lack of correlation, except in terms of appropriate levels, between these two dynamics. An illustration may be of help: When a local congregation improves its parking spaces, it lowers the level of dissatisfaction that people have had about inadequate parking. But until that congregation and pastor improve the corporate and dynamic character of worship, the level of satisfaction will not be raised. To be sure, there may be a momentary sense of satisfaction within the congregation that it has, at last, improved parking. But unless the service of worship speaks powerfully and caringly to people's human hurts and hopes, the level of satisfaction will continue to be essentially what it is.

It is precisely because of this operative principle about levels of satisfaction and dissatisfaction that it is important for a congregation to nurture and put well in place a greater number of the relational characteristics than the functional characteristics. The diagnostic approach to long-range planning for mission here encourages a local church to measure its priorities thoughtfully and assess its strengths in terms of these relational and functional characteristics of substantial missional churches. As a church discovers its missional priorities and its present strengths, it can build on these for the future.

Long Range Planning Is Strategic

Effective, successful congregations claim their present foundational strengths, expand these strengths in decisive ways, and add new foundational strengths that contribute to shaping the future and destiny of the congregation. The three most strategic decisions in long-range planning are found in the key words—*claim, expand, add.*

Claim Your Strengths

The first strategic decision in successful long-range planning is to help a congregation to find and claim its present central strengths. Realistically knowing and strongly affirming those strengths that the church "has going for it" is decisive for success. Substantial power is generated as a congregation discovers and claims its strengths: Power for the future is found in claiming our strengths, not in focusing on our weaknesses and shortcomings.

From the perspective of the Bible, it is consequential that a church first decide its strengths. They are present precisely because God has enabled His people to develop them. In a sense, a church that denies its strengths denies God. A church that decides to claim its strengths affirms that the power of God has been at work in the congregation, enabling it to develop these specific strengths. It is not on an "ego trip." In a genuine sense, these strengths are gifts from God, and as gifts, they now belong to the congregation. With God's giving and compassionate power, the congregation has nurtured these strengths. To claim them is to claim the compelling presence of God's power.

Thus, helping a congregation to claim its strengths is not a simplistic exercise in positive thinking. It is not some sham to fool a church into thinking it is "doing all right." It is not a false optimism, like whistling in the dark to give a pretense of confidence.

Successful long-range planning begins with helping a church claim its strengths precisely *because* long-range planning begins with God. Regrettably, much long-range planning begins by focusing on the needs, weaknesses, failures, and shortcomings of a congregation. Many congregations ask the wrong first questions: "What are our needs? What are our problems?"

These are the wrong questions with which to begin, for two reasons. First, the questions deny what God has already shared with the congregation. Second, they are egocentric in their focus. They focus on *our* needs and *our* problems rather than on what God is calling us to do.

The strategic questions for successful long-range planning are

1. What are our present foundational strengths, given from God?
2. How can these strengths be expanded to serve God's mission more effectively?
3. Which foundational strengths can be added, that we might more successfully serve God's mission?

The key decisions in long-range planning are the decisions to (1) claim,

(2) expand, and (3) add to the congregation's strengths, and they are achieved with the compelling vision that God is calling this congregation to accomplish effective, successful mission.

Expand Your Strengths

Once a congregation has claimed its strengths, it is strategic that it decide on new ways to expand these strengths. It is decisive in successful long-range planning that a congregation build on its strengths, not its weaknesses. When a church expands its strengths, gifts, graces, and talents, it becomes more effective in mission. When it becomes preoccupied with its weaknesses, it begins to lose its strengths. Strengths that are not used weaken and decay.

A church must "run to its strengths." In professional football, for a winning team to run to its strengths means that a team that has an all-pro right guard, right tackle, right end, and right halfback will run to its right—that is, run to its strengths. Too many churches with strengths at "right guard, right tackle, right end, and right half-back" spend too much time trying to run plays around left end. They wonder why they do not have many "winning games." They run to their weaknesses rather than to their strengths.

A church with a deeply inspirational worship service would do well to expand its visitation program inviting people to worship before it tries to start a recreational ministry. A congregation with strong outreach to alcoholics would do well to expand its ministry to the families of alcoholics before it tries to start a ministry for parents without partners. A church with an active visitation program to members would do well to expand to visiting unchurched persons before it tries to start a Sunday School class for single young adults.

A church with an effective adult choir might well start a children's choir. A church with a solid youth program might participate in a summer community softball league. A church with a successful visitation ministry in hospitals might well expand to a strong ministry with shut-ins and their families. In constructive, creative ways effective churches expand—build on—their present foundational strengths.

This principle is sound with people and groups as well. The most effective way to help people with their hurts and hopes is to help them build on their present strengths—to claim and expand the competencies and gifts, however meager, that they now have. As they build on their strengths, they will gain the confidence to deal with their weakness and shortcomings.

Note that this approach does not ignore or deny the existence of needs and problems, weaknesses and shortcomings. Rather, it takes seriously the difficult reality of these weaknesses. Strategic long-range planning is committed to the approach that weaknesses are most effectively dealt with as one builds on one's present strengths.

Add New Strengths

Strategic long-range planning further includes helping a congregation to decide which new foundational strengths to add that are commensurate with and build on those already in place. A professional football team with an all-pro right guard, right tackle, right end, and right halfback would do well to add an all-pro center or left guard rather than a left end. That is, new strengths should build on present strengths in substantial, supplementary ways.

Many churches misunderstand this fundamental principle. Regrettably, they do a "fill the gaps" approach to developing their future. They focus on their weaknesses and rush around busily trying to fill all the gaps. They imagine that all the gaps must be filled this year or next, and thus, they try to do too much too soon. They set themselves up for failure, and then they become preoccupied with their new-found failures. In the process, they lose sight of their strengths and end up in poorer condition than when they began.

The art of long-range planning is to decide those few strategic new strengths that it makes sense to add in the coming five to seven years. Successful churches work smarter, not harder. Of ten objectives that a church might work toward, two will be decisive in shaping that church's future. The other eight objectives will be helpful and useful; the central two will be strategic and decisive.

Strategic long-range planning takes seriously the fact that a few critical activities achieve most of the results produced by an organization. This truth was first set forth by Vilfredo Pareto, a nineteenth-century Italian economist. It was frequently stated by Pareto as follows: Eighty percent of the value lies in 20 percent of the elements, while the remaining 20 percent of the value lies in the remaining 80 percent of the elements. This is referred to as the Twenty-Eighty Rule.

That is to say, 20 percent of the objectives toward which a congregation heads will yield 80 percent of the results for that congregation, and 80 percent of the objectives they develop will yield 20 percent of the results. The art of strategic long-range planning is to focus on the 20 percent that will accomplish most of the results. Congregations frequently develop thirty or forty objectives in a long-range planning session. The art of strategic long-range planning is to select the six out of thirty worthwhile objectives that will be strategically decisive and that, in fact, will yield 80 percent of the results for that congregation.

In adding new strengths, therefore, it is important that a church decide those few key strengths (1) that build on and supplement their present strengths, and (2) that will be strategically decisive in advancing that particular church's future and destiny.

Long-Range Planning Is Responsibly Hopeful

Effective long-range planning builds on a God-given hope that is (1) responsible and realistic, (2) courageous and compassionate, and (3) prayerful and powerful. In the church, long-range planning takes seriously that the God of Abraham, Isaac, Jacob, and Moses goes before His people as a cloud by day and a fire by night—leading them through this present wilderness toward the future He has prepared for His people. Long-range planning takes seriously the open tomb and risen Lord of the Easter faith.

To be sure, long-range planning appropriately studies sociological and demographic trends. It is useful that we consider such data projections, but it is vital that we not become slaves to them in our decisions. Many so-called trends are simply self-fulfilling prophecies. That is, they come true only because enough people believe they will come true. Hence, they behave, act, and make decisions in such a fashion that they contribute to the trend running its predicted course.

Effective long-range planning must raise serious questions as to whether certain so-called trends in a county should be allowed to come to pass. For example, certain people once projected that a given county would likely lose population, jobs, and school funds over a ten-year period. Enough people, businesses, and teachers believed the projections so that a quiet exodus began—and the trend came to pass.

In another county, the same so-called projections were put forward. A pastor, a businessman, and a community leader did not believe the future had to be that way. In a realistic, courageous, and prayerful fashion, they set out to change the projected future of their county. The struggle was, in fact, enormous. New industry did come. New school funds were developed. New jobs were created. New people did move in. Other people—planning to move—decided to stay. The quality of life in the county did improve.

Now, it will not always happen this way. But Christians—doing strategic long-range planning—rely finally on God, not data projections. This reliance on God is responsible and realistic, not foolhardy and stupid. We are called, not to march blindly off the cliff, but to build a bridge to the other side.

This reliance on God—in hope—is courageous and compassionate, not timid and calculating. Too many churches do long-range planning in "safe," "comfortable" ways. God does not call us to stay by the Red Sea. He calls us to follow Him into the wilderness. And He calls us to a mission that invites us to be our most creative, constructive, compassionate selves. We are, in point of fact, called to be good shepherds in this world. That does mean seeking out those who are lost.

This reliance on God is prayerful and powerful. It is strange to me that so many long-range planning committees do not pray. They study statistics and charts. They draw up long lists of problems and needs. They fail to see the strengths that God has provided them. They discuss their options for the future more like amateur sociologists than "called-of-God Christians." And they wonder why they fail.

Effective long-range planning builds on a God-given hope that is prayerful and powerful. In prayerful ways—open to God's power—the long-range planning committee genuinely prays, "What is God calling us to do—as His people?" And, though our vision may focus on the coming five to seven to ten years, our eyes look even beyond these time horizons to all that God is preparing for us in the whole of the future yet to come. There is power in the steady, solid confidence of this vision.

The watershed question for many people in many congregations is: Do you believe that your best years are behind you, or do you believe that your best years are yet before you? Some churches believe that their best years are behind them. Some people believe that their best years have been. They behave and act as though the future will be less than that which has passed. And it is precisely because they behave and act that way that the future for them turns out to *be* less than that which has been.

Effective, successful churches live in the confidence of God's promise that some of their best years are yet to come. In Revelation 21:5 these words are found: "And He who sat upon the throne said, 'Behold, I make all things new.' " This does not mean that the future will become progressively better and better. Rather, it means that amidst the pain, suffering, and tragedies that lie before us in our future, God goes before us to make all things new—inviting us to that future that he has both promised and prepared for us. God is not simply in the past. God is in the present and the future leading and drawing us toward newness of life.

Hope is stronger than memory. Salvation is stronger than sin. Forgiveness is stronger than bitterness. Reconciliation is stronger than hatred. Resurrection is stronger than crucifixion. Light is stronger than darkness. . . . Hope is stronger than memory.

Introduction, Part II:
Mission and Success

In the coming years, we need more churches that are interested in success and fewer churches that are preoccupied with their own problems. We need more churches committed to effective mission and fewer churches caught in the web of their own shortcomings and needs. We need more churches that are planning for mission and success and fewer that are frozen in their own weaknesses and failures.

The dark malaise of the Christian church in our time is that so many congregations have developed a preoccupation with their weaknesses, their problems, and their concerns. It is as if there were no open tomb or risen Lord. It is as if these congregations preferred to live locked in a closed tomb, focusing on their past and refusing to recognize the strengths God has shared with them that they might be in mission in this world.

Our hope in the years before us is in competency and mission, not in commitment and professional ministry. We need more persons who are willing to be competent, compassionate, courageous, and committed missionaries, and we need fewer who are willing to be only professional ministers. That is to say, we need more persons who are willing to be active in the world in mission and fewer who are willing to be only *re*active within the programs and activities of the local church.

We who live in the United States live in one of the richest, most promising mission fields on the planet Earth. This is not the churched culture of bygone days—of thirty years ago, of the 1950s. In vast ranges of this country, 50 to 60 percent of the population, depending on the section of the country, is unchurched. The range of human hurts and hopes that cry out for mission is enormous. Regrettably, many of our churches grow despair, fragmentation, and loneliness better than they nurture hope, reconciliation, caring, and justice.

We need more churches willing to be "churches of the Good Shepherd." We need fewer churches that are "Bo-Peep churches." Bo-Peep churches do pretty well precisely what the poem indicates:

> *Little Bo Peep has lost her sheep*
> *and doesn't know where to find them.*
> *But leave them alone and they'll come home*
> *wagging their tails behind them.*

Too many churches have taken this stance with the scores of unchurched people across this land. They have become the Bo-Peep churches of a Mother Goose land that does not see the hurts and hopes that call for effective mission.

By contrast, we need more churches that are willing to be churches of the Good Shepherd. In the biblical narrative, Jesus refers to the Good Shepherd as the one who—with ninety-nine sheep in the fold— went out into the rough, rocky places to seek out that one sheep that was lost. Our predicament—indeed, our opportunity and our mission—is that with fifty sheep in the fold, there are fifty who are lost in the rough and rocky places of life. Churches in our time are called to effective mission in sharing help with the tough hurts and hopes present among our people.

In strategic long-range planning for a local congregation, four steps are important for effective, successful mission to take place:

1. Develop a realistic assessment of its present standing and stature in relation to other congregations.
2. Make fundamental decisions as to the primary direction for its future.
3. Study its strengths in relation to the central characteristics of effective, successful churches.
4. Decide those strategic objectives that will advance its long-range effectiveness in mission.

By following these steps, it will be possible for a local congregation to develop thoughtful decisions that build on that congregation's central strengths and enable it to be decisively in mission in its community.

Frequently, a long-range planning committee is given the responsibility to lead the congregation through these four key steps. At the conclusion of its work, such a committee would do well to organize its own recommendations into three groups: present foundational strengths; foundational strengths to be expanded; and foundational strengths to be added in the future. That is to say, effective, successful mission must build on those foundational strengths that are well in place, those that will be expanded, and those that are to be added in the coming five to seven years.

In this Introduction, steps 1 and 2 will be discussed in some detail. Much of the rest of the book is devoted to helping the reader gain a better understanding of the central characteristics of effective congregations, step 3. Step 4 is discussed in the concluding chapter.

Two observations are useful at this juncture. First, strategic long-range planning takes seriously a strong theology of mission and an abiding conviction that God is deeply present in the life and mission of a congregation: God is the source of a congregation's strengths. God's calling invites a congregation to be in effective mission. God's compelling compassion sustains a congregation as it moves forward to achieve in the direction to which God has called the congregation.

Second, strategic long-range planning takes seriously the study of regional dynamics in relation to substantial community developments, population-church analysis, and emerging groupings for mission. So much work has been done in the field of demographic analysis that this material will not be recapitulated in this book. My contribution to the life and mission of congregations focuses on a thoughtful analysis of the central characteristics of effective churches.

Realistic Assessment of Standing and Stature

As the first step in long-range planning, it is important that the long-range planning committee and the congregation as a whole develop an accurate, realistic assessment of their present standing and stature as a local church in comparison with other congregations. The major indicators are:

average attendance at worship services
average attendance at church school
church school enrollment
church membership

These indicators are listed in the order of their importance. The "participation" indicators of worship attendance and church school attendance are more indicative of the vitality and strength of a local church than are the "membership" indicators of church school enrollment and church membership.

Many churches have an inaccurate assessment of their present standing; generally, they think they are smaller than they really are. Frequently, they think more poorly of themselves than they have a right to think. To be sure, they ought not to think better of themselves than they have a right to do so, but they should have a realistic assessment of how they compare to other local churches.

P → B → D: that is, Perception yields Behavior yields Destiny. Local churches that are middle-sized congregations based on the indicators but think they are "small" tend to behave and act as though they were small. Give them enough time, and their destiny will be to become small. This is one reason there are so many "stable and declining" local churches across the country. Even though a local church is middle-sized, if its perception is that it is small, it will develop the size of its mission *below* its capacities and it will "grow" downward to the size of mission it has set for itself. It is decisive, therefore, that a local church begin its long-range planning with a realistic assessment of its present standing and stature.

Figure I.1 Assessment of Present Standing and Stature

Is this congregation a large congregation, a middle-sized congregation, a small congregation?

Draw a line in each of the four graphs below to indicate your church's present standing in relation to United Methodist churches. (Given a variation of a percentile or two, these figures are essentially the same for many Protestant denominations.) For example, if your average attendance at worship services is 74, draw a line under the 50–74 figure, and then circle the corresponding percentile figure, which would be 57.5. This would mean that your church's average attendance at worship services is higher than that of 57.5% of all United Methodist churches.

Average Attendance of Worship Services	Total % of Churches	Average Attendance at Church School	Total % of Church Schools	Church School Enrollment	Total % of Church Schools	Church Membership	Total % of Churches
1000+	99.7	500+	100.1	1000+	99.9	3000+	100.0
750–999	99.6	300–499	99.8	750–999	99.4	2000–2999	99.9
500–749	99.3	200–299	98.8	500–749	98.9	1500–1999	99.4
350–499	98.4	150–199	96.5	400–499	97.4	1000–1499	98.6
200–349	96.3	125–149	93.2	300–399	95.9	750–999	96.3
150–199	88.6	100–124	90.0	250–299	93.0	500–749	93.4
100–149	81.6	75–99	85.0	200–249	90.4	300–499	87.4
75–99	69.1	50–74	75.6	150–199	86.3	200–299	76.2
50–74	57.5	35–49	58.3	100–149	78.8	100–199	64.6
35–49	40.5	25–34	41.3	75–99	64.6	50–99	41.4
20–34	26.7	15–24	27.2	50–74	52.3	1–49	19.1
1–19	10.9	1–14	11.7	25–49	35.2		
				1–24	12.7		

Source: Department of Statistics, General Council on Finance and Administration of the United Methodist Church.

The Primary Direction for the Local Church's Future

The second step is for the long-range planning committee to make a tentative decision as to the primary direction for their local church's future. This "primary direction" entails tentative decisions regarding:

1. the maximum mission potential available to them in their community
2. the total number of people—members, constituents, and persons served in mission—that their church plans to serve each year during the coming five to seven years
3. the fundamental type of church they want to become

With regard to a local church's maximum mission potential, most churches need to be realistic as to the number of people available with which to be in mission. In sparsely populated areas such as west Texas, for example, the maximum mission potential may be only five persons who are unchurched within forty-five minutes driving time. There are lots of cattle and cactus, scorpions and snakes—and very few people. Most churches are not in west Texas—and they have considerable mission potential. Indeed, our country is one of the richest mission fields on the planet. Nationally, 50 percent of the population is effectively unchurched. God has placed us in a major mission field and called us to be His good shepherds in this time and place.

With regard to the "total number of people served each year," most churches are helping more people each year than they sometimes realize. It is sad that ministers and church leaders think of the size of their church only in terms of how many members it has. Churches need to see the help they give to constituents (nonmembers who participate in church activities) and persons served in mission in the community. And they need to make a thoughtful, intentional decision as to the total number of people they *plan* to help—"the Lord willing and the creeks don't rise"—each year. Perhaps the Lord wills that we help even when the creeks do rise.

With regard to the "fundamental type of church" we intend to be, the long-range planning committee appropriately makes a conscious decision as to the primary direction for our local church's future. There are five types of churches:

1. rapidly growing
2. stable and growing
3. stable
4. stable and declining
5. dying

Except in a few isolated geographical regions of the country, most churches can decide which type of church they want to be in the future. Given their maximum mission potential and the total number of people they plan to help each year, they will, in fact, have decided the primary direction and type of church they will become.

Two formulas are helpful in enabling a local congregation to decide the outer limits of the primary direction for its future. The first of these is the Maximum Mission Potential Formula.

1.   This formula is shown as a worksheet in Figure I.2. These basic points about the formula will be helpful to your understanding it. Average trip time (1) refers to the amount of time people invest in traveling to work, to do major shopping, and to participate in major social and recreational activities. Average trip time does not refer to the amount of time people invest in driving to church; rather, it refers to the amount of time they spend in everyday life in an average trip. Each community has its own "time horizons."

In major metropolitian areas of the country the average trip time is thirty minutes or more. In small towns the average trip time may be five to ten minutes. The point is that people will tend to invest in driving to church essentially the same, but, generally speaking, no more than, the amount of time they invest in an average trip during the course of a week.

2.   Technically speaking, the total population within average trip time radius of a given congregation is its primary mission field. It is important that a church be in mission with the hurts and hopes that are present within that total population. At the same time, it is important that a church take seriously the geographical barriers, community boundaries, and major traffic patterns that will influence their capacity to be in mission with given groups of people.

3.   Significant geographical barriers are rivers, mountains, major expressways, and so on; generally speaking, they decisively influence the mission field of a given church. Community boundaries are those visible and invisible boundaries that shape the direction and pattern of people's lives; for example, there is a dotted line on a map that indicates the line between Morgan Country and Smith County. People tend to live on either side of that dotted line because, in fact, it is a strong community boundary.

Traffic directional patterns are the way in which people move about in day-to-day life. People tend to go to church along the traffic patterns they follow in the course of an ordinary week. To put that another way, people who drive from north to south to work, with an average trip time of thirty minutes, are more likely to drive from north to south to a church that is located twenty to thirty minutes from their house. They are less likely to drive from south to north to a church that is only ten minutes

Figure I.2   Maximum Mission Potential Formula

	Now	*Projected 10 Years Ahead*
1. Compute average trip time (ATT) in your community.	_____	_____
2. Calculate total population within ATT radius of your church.	_____	_____
3. Adjust for significant geographical barriers, community boundaries, and major traffic directional patterns.	_____	_____
4. Calculate 50% of the adjusted total population (from step 3) to discover effectively unchurched population within ATT of your church. (Use 60% or 70% if there is a greater density of unchurched population.)	_____	_____
5. Compute 15% of unchurched population (from step 4) to discover homogeneous potential for mission. *Note:* Use 20% for homogeneous areas of the country and 10% for heterogeneous areas.	_____	_____
6. For realistic Maximum Mission Potential, increase homogeneous unchurched population figure (from step 5) by 20% based on the principle of homogeneity and heterogeneity. (Use 30% if the local church has an extraordinary commitment *and* a substantial percentage of the community is unchurched.)	_____	_____

from their house. There are many exceptions to that basic principle, but, again and again, I have found that people tend to live out their lives in dominant traffic direction patterns.

The formula invites the local church to adjust the total population figure by at least 50 percent. In some parts of the country with a higher proportion of unchurched people, it will be important to adjust the population figure by 60 or 70 percent, depending on an estimate of the number of unchurched people within that community. It should be noted that the unchurched population is people who are not—even minimally—participants in the life and mission of any congregation.

5. The basic figure for computing the homogeneous potential for mission is 15 percent. The more homogeneous the region of the country, the more it would be helpful to use 20 percent. The more heterogeneous the area under consideration, the more likely a 10 percent figure will be accurate.

6. The church growth movement has focused very strongly on the principle of homogeneity. I reject that principle as the only principle on which to engage in mission and develop church growth. Hence the formula asks that step 6 be computed. That is, the formula invites an increase of the figure from step 5 by at least 20 percent. It would be appropriate to increase the figure by 30 percent wherever two factors are present: (1) the local congregation has an extraordinary commitment to mission in the community, and (2) a substantial percentage of the community is unchurched.

The second formula is the Mission-Constituent-Member Formula. Basically this formula affirms that there are three kinds of people when one considers the primary direction of a church's future. First, there are *persons served in mission.* These are individuals in the community, neither constituents nor members, who are intentionally ministered to in terms of their human hopes and hurts, in the name of Christ and on behalf of that local congregation. There is some direct linkage between that local congregation, its pastor and/or laypersons, and those who are served in mission.

The second group is *constituents*—that is, nonmembers who participate more than once in one or more activities of the church in a six-month period. Churches usually have far more constituents than they are aware of.

The third group is *members,* and for purposes of this formula, members are defined as resident members who are marginally active to fully active in the life and mission of the local church. Nonresident members and inactive members are not included in this basic formula.

It is important to note that, in the unchurched culture in which we currently live, people are more likely to first be persons served in mission. Then some of them will decide to become constituents, and then some of those will decide to become members. Those churches who work on the membership column are working on the wrong column.

To use business terminology, members are stockholders, constituents are regular and occasional customers, and persons served in mission are

Figure I.3   Mission-Constituent-Member Formula

Type of Church	Members	Constituents	Persons Served in Mission
Rapidly growing	100	125	100
Stable and growing	100	100	75
Stable	100	75	50
Stable and declining	100	50	25
Dying	100	25	10

For example, based on a conservative analysis, a stable and growing church tends to have 100 constituents and be in mission with 75 persons in the community for each 100 resident, reasonably active members.

DEFINITIONS

Members: resident members who are marginally active to fully active in the life and mission of the church. Nonresident members and inactive members should not be included.

Constituents: nonmembers who are participating in one or more activities of the church 2–4 times or more in a six-month period.

Persons served in mission: those individuals in the community, neither constituents nor members, who are intentionally ministered to in terms of their human hopes and hurts.

the client pool. Churches that prefer to be stable and declining will focus most of their energy and effort on stockholders. No business that seeks to be stable and growing would invest the majority of its energy and resources on stockholders. Indeed, the art of making a solid business grow is that of effectively serving the range of people who are in the client pool. Some of these will become regular and occasional customers and some of those will become stockholders. A person who is currently active in a given church generally has decided to become active because that church had extended its helping missional outreach with regard to his human hurts and hopes.

The Congregation's Strengths in Relation to the Central Characteristics of Effective, Successful Churches

The third step is for the long-range planning committee to do a thoughtful, diagnostic study of the key strengths of the local church. Most effective, successful churches have substantially developed nine or more of the twelve central characteristics. The task of the long-range

Figure I.4 The Central Characteristics of Successful Churches

The purpose of this chart is to help you discover those characteristics that are central *strengths* of your local church. If you think your church rates an 8, 9, or 10 on a given characteristic, circle the appropriate number. (Please note that 10 is the highest ranking.) After you have done so, underline those characteristics rated 8, 9, or 10. Do not rank all twelve characteristics now—only those you regard as 8, 9, or 10.

Relational Characteristics

1. Specific, Concrete Missional Objectives
    1 2 3 4 5 6 7 8 9 10

2. Pastoral/Lay Visitation in Community
    1 2 3 4 5 6 7 8 9 10

3. Corporate, Dynamic Worship
    1 2 3 4 5 6 7 8 9 10

4. Significant Relational Groups
    1 2 3 4 5 6 7 8 9 10

5. Strong Leadership Resources
    1 2 3 4 5 6 7 8 9 10

6. Solid, Participatory Decision Making
    1 2 3 4 5 6 7 8 9 10

Functional Characteristics

7. Several Competent Programs and Activities
    1 2 3 4 5 6 7 8 9 10

8. Open Accessibility
    1 2 3 4 5 6 7 8 9 10

9. High Visibility
    1 2 3 4 5 6 7 8 9 10

10. Adequate Parking
    1 2 3 4 5 6 7 8 9 10

11. Adequate Space and Facilities
    1 2 3 4 5 6 7 8 9 10

12. Solid Financial Resources
    1 2 3 4 5 6 7 8 9 10

planning committee is to assess each of these twelve characteristics in this local church and decide which ones may be rated 8, 9, or 10.

In a preliminary way, the long-range planning committee can use the chart in Figure I.4 to decide which of the twelve are well in place as 8, 9, or 10 in this congregation. The committee may want to invite additional persons in the church to contribute their thoughts by filling in the chart as well.

In its preliminary work, it is valuable for the committee to focus on only those characteristics in their local church that can be rated as 8, 9, or 10. The committee should not at this point evaluate its ranking on each of the twelve characteristics. Their initial task is to come to some consensus on which ones are current central strengths for this church.

After this preliminary assessment, it is appropriate that the long-range planning committee consider each of the twelve characteristics in depth. The following chapters are designed to facilitate this study.

1. Specific, Concrete Missional Objectives

Human Hurts and Hopes

A successful church delivers effective missional outreach, shepherding of its families and friends through life's pilgrimage, primary groups of sharing and caring, corporate and prayerful worship, and a thoughtful, streamlined organizational structure—all toward developing the congregation's mission in the world, growth in grace, and understanding of everyday life in the light of the Christian faith. Decisive to the genuine success of any congregation is its capacity to share substantive mission in the world.

Indeed, the first and most central characteristic of an effective, successful church is its specific, concrete, missional objectives.

"Specific" refers to the fact that the local congregation has focused its missional outreach on a particular human hurt and hope—for example, by being in mission with alcoholics and their families, with homebound elderly, or with epileptics and their families. Missional outreach is not best accomplished by developing a purpose statement or some generalized approach to a given age group in the surrounding area. Nor is mission best accomplished by the church seeking to engage in helping everyone with everything. The church that does that ends up helping no one with anything.

Missional Objectives

Those churches that have been effective in missional outreach have tended to identify very specific human hurts and hopes with which they have shared their principal leadership and financial resources. It is important that a church not try to attain too many specific, concrete missional objectives. Indeed, it would be advisable to focus on only one, two, or three such objectives.

"Concrete" refers to the local church's delivering of effective help, hope, and new life in a competent, compassionate, committed, and courageous manner. Developing a statement of purpose is not delivering effective mission; it is simply developing a statement of purpose. Neither does preaching a series of sermons about the compelling value of being engaged in missional outreach mean that a church has been doing missional outreach. The scriptural references speak of very concrete forms of help, like feeding the hungry, clothing the naked, giving shelter. That is to say, mission happens only when effective help has been delivered—until that consequential sharing of effective help has occurred, no mission has taken place.

*   "Missional" refers to the fact that in doing effective mission, the local congregation focuses on both individual as well as institutional hurts and hopes. Some congregations limit their missional concern to helping only individuals. Other congregations limit their missional concern by focusing on institutional and corporate issues in society, and on the policies and programs persistent in the culture. Limitation of mission either to self or to societal issues is inappropriate. It is not possible to help individuals genuinely and effectively without also taking seriously societal dynamics that impinge upon the plight of the individual. Likewise, it is not possible to wrestle with the grave societal issues of the culture without delivering effective help to the individuals/groups comprising that culture.

*   "Objectives" refers to missional direction stated in a sufficiently clear fashion that it is possible to know when they have been achieved. Those missional objectives may be stated in informal or formal ways. The local congregation that is effective in mission is the congregation that has a compelling passion for the achievement and accomplishment of mission and has moved forward toward the substantial accomplishment and achievement of very clear, intentional goals. The effective congregation is not engaged in wishful thinking with a generalized purpose or goal statement that lists just its sentiments to do something noble, worthwhile, and helpful.

The five M's of the Christian church are Mission, Management, Members, Money, and Maintenance. That is their appropriate and rightful order. Mission comes before all else. Management is the wise and courageous development and deployment of the Members and the Money—that is, the leadership and the financial resources—toward effective Mission. The fifth M—Maintenance—is what we do when we have worn ourselves out in Mission. Indeed, the more effective a congregation is in mission, the easier it is for that congregation to deal with issues of maintenance. Conversely, the more preoccupied a congregation is with maintenance, the less likely it is to have the strength and resources to deal effectively with maintenance—let alone be responsibly and creatively engaged in mission.

Regrettably, in many of the churches of our country there is a preoccupation with membership. A simple illustration will suffice: Two ministers meet at a conference. The one minister is in the process of moving to a new pastorate. The other minister, in an almost automatic way, asks,

"How many members does your new church have?" The more important question would be, "How many people is your new church serving in mission?"

Mission leads us beyond ourselves. Whenever a local congregation is effectively engaged in missional outreach, that congregation is a group of people living beyond their preoccupation with themselves. Precisely because they live beyond themselves, their strengths are commensurately developed, their vision is substantially lifted, and their energies are vitalized to new levels of living.

Some people think that large churches are great churches. Some people think that the more members a church has, the greater that church is. Pastors are frequently heard to speak of a given church as being one of the greatest churches in the country; more often than not, they're describing essentially a large church. But the great churches in Christendom are those that have learned the art of accepting "unacceptable persons."

In the eyes of God no person is unacceptable; with our dimmer vision, we frequently think of persons and groups around us as unacceptable. One reason I stand so strongly against the principle of homogeneity as the primary source of church growth is that it invites the attitude that the art of church growth is that of reaching out to people who are essentially acceptable. We are called of Christ to accept those who are acceptable and we are called of Christ to accept those whom we—with our limited vision—imagine are *un*acceptable.

One way of breaking down a local church's preoccupation with homogeneity is for two or three of the leaders in that congregation to learn the art of loving the "black sheep" in their own families. Even in the most homogeneous of families, there are those who have been labeled as black sheep. As we learn the art of accepting those whom we think are unacceptable, we learn the art of being—in the best sense—a great church.

Generally, an effective local church has one, two, or three major objectives in the local community. That is, the congregation delivers concrete help to one, two, or three specific hurts and hopes. If a church has five to eight major missional objectives it probably has too many. An excellent exercise for leaders of a congregation is to do the following:

1. List up to three present *major* missional objectives that your local church is accomplishing in your community.
2. List up to three *major* missional objectives that are planned for the coming five years by key leaders and groups in your church as they seek to reach out in the community.
3. List any possible *major* missional objectives that are being given future consideration.

The church that, on a scale of 1 to 10, is an 8, 9, or 10 is the church that is able to list one or two present major missional objectives, one major missional objective that is already planned for implementation in the coming five years, and perhaps one additional major missional objective that is being given consideration for the future.

Two points are important to note. First, I am not suggesting that people who have specific human hurts and hopes be turned away simply because a local congregation does not have that specific hurt or hope as a part of their present or proposed or possible missional objectives. Major missional objectives are those present, proposed, and possible objectives for which we are investing or plan to invest substantial leadership and financial resources. Certainly, we would have a range of minor missional accomplishments during the course of a given year. But it is important for a congregation to creatively and constructively channel its leadership and financial resources toward a few specific missional objectives.

Secondly, there is the spillover effect. When a local congregation is effective in delivering concrete help to a specific hurt or hope, it is likely to be sought out by people in the community who have other hurts and hopes. The spillover effect occurs when the community grapevine spreads the word that a church effectively helped someone, for example, with alcoholism. Hearing this, some people might hope that they can be helped with their struggles with dealing with chronic illness or with developing career objectives or with developing a solid values system. The more a local church diversifies, trying to help everybody with everything, the more it gets the reputation through the community grapevine of helping nobody with anything, because that's precisely what it will end up doing. Its human and financial resources will be so fragmented and scattered that it will not finally deliver substantial, effective help for any one major human hurt or hope.

Another dimension of the spillover effect is important to note: The more a congregation strengthens its competency and capacity to help with a specific human hurt and hope, the more its capacities are developed to share help with other specific human hurts and hopes. The more people there are in the congregation who have learned the art of helping in relation to a specific hurt and hope, the more likely those people are to have the competence and confidence to share help as others seek them out or, indeed, as they intentionally and caringly seek others out.

Growing Mission Up

In many local churches, the most effective way to develop mission is to "grow it up from within." By inviting members of a congregation to look within themselves at their own longings and strengths to help, it becomes possible to grow the church's mission forward from within.

The theological perspective out of which this approach of growing a mission up from within develops is based upon these convictions: First, I am convinced that God places specific longings to help in each human heart. That is, within each person are specific affinities to share help toward given human hurts and hopes to which they are attracted because of their deep longings toward them. Secondly, God shares concrete strengths and resources to enable the helper to be reasonably effective in mission. That is, God is the provider of the competencies and capacities that enable a person to share help with those individuals who have a human hurt and hope commensurate with the helper's own specific longings. Thirdly, God helps us discover persons with similiar longings and strengths. Fourthly, God's action in the world helps us to see that a specific missional outreach is timely and important. Lastly, God calls us to invest our longings and strengths in this life's pilgrimage in competent, compassionate, committed, and courageous ways.

Unfortunately, a number of churches try to develop mission by looking "out there" for societal problems and then planning to do mission "from the top down." This approach is both unproductive and frustrating. Further, the lack of success tends to create a sense of self-righteousness, in that people within that congregation say, "Well, at least we tried, and we can't help it if it didn't work out." Looking first at what is out there in society in the way of problems is looking first in the wrong direction.

It is worth noting that effective missional outreach does not normally come forth from planning retreats, board meetings, or long-range planning committees. More often than not, mission simply grows itself up because a small number of people—three to five—have discovered similar longings to help with a specific human hurt and hope. Growing from their longings, that missional outreach blossoms and develops into a full-range mission in the community.

This is not to deny the planning capabilities of boards or retreats or long-range planning committees. These groups do possess the strengths and capabilities required for developing missional objectives, but they are often focused on generalized mission statements or on looking at the problems in the community. These efforts often become stagnant and unproductive when they emerge out of an artificial attempt to construct mission. People do not often develop missional objectives in the vacuum of purpose statements, or in looking at "what's out there in the community."

Perhaps you've been on a committee that was taught, and rightly so, from the pulpit that the church must be in mission. You and your fellow committee members then felt pressed to become more "mission-minded." As a result, there was an effort to force missional goals into being. "Well, we need to be in mission. That's what the church ought to be about. Let's see what we can come up with." To prevent this, both the pastor and the committee need a fuller understanding of how mission has grown itself up historically in the Christian church.

Generally speaking, mission has grown itself up when three factors have converged:

1. One or more persons have discovered their longings—their compelling compassion—to share help with a given hurt and hope.
2. They have discovered their strength and the caring strength of three to five others who have similar longings.
3. Events within the community have occurred that make the sharing of those strengths and longings imperative now.

Consider your own responses to the five invitational questions that are important as you think through the mission to which God is calling you. The first, central question is, What specific human hurts and hopes do you have longings to help with?

A useful way to discover your own longings to help is to think through what specific hurt and hope keeps you awake at night upon occasion. That is, in those moments when you are seeking to fall asleep but can't quite do so because you are preoccupied with some person and their hurt and hope, what is the shape of that hurt and hope and who is the person you long to help? That will give you a clue as to where your longings are. A further clue can be discovered as you think about those occasions when you were driving down the road or waiting somewhere and your mind drifted to a given person and their hurt and hope. Think through the distinctive character of that hurt and hope. These are clues as to where your own interests and longings might be.

The principle is clear and forthright: Missional objectives start with a longing to help, and people sometimes discover that longing to help as they lie awake at night, restless and disturbed. Mission starts with people like you and me. When a human hurt and hope becomes compelling for three to five people who have discovered common longings and strengths, a missional objective has come into being.

The second invitational question related to mission is, What concrete strengths do you have with which to share effective help for these specific human hurts and hopes? Missional objectives are nurtured by the strengths, compassion, and caring of a small group in a congregation, who respond to hurts and hopes out of their own God-given longings to help. Some persons are able to empathize with the problems of a young single parent family more readily than with the problems of a home-bound older adult. You understand and have compassion toward certain specific dilemmas in life; your own pilgrimage of life has brought on given hurts and hopes that enable you to share and care more effectively in similiar kinds of situations.

Sometimes a given person, group of people, or congregation will have longings to help with a number of hurts and hopes. Whenever that is the case, the wise thing to do is to choose those longings for which you have commensurate strengths to deliver effective help. Now, this is not to discount our being in mission out of our weaknesses. Sometimes God calls us to deliver effective help in relation to longings for which we have no commensurate competency and strength. We are simply called to share even out of our weaknesses. But the basic conviction that we should match our strengths and longings is to affirm that strength-based mission is an important first step toward developing one's competency and capacity to do effective mission. As we develop the experience of having accomplished effective mission growing out of our longings and our strengths, we are in a better position to share effective mission even as it grows out of our weaknesses.

 The third invitational question concerning effective mission is, What three to five persons do you know who have similiar longings and strengths in your church or in your community? Isolated and individualistic approaches to mission are unproductive. It is important that the person who has discovered longings and strengths look around and discover others with similiar longings and strengths. We are called to be in mission corporately, not individually. There are too many pastors who see themselves as "Lone Rangers." Indeed, it is worth pointing out that even the Lone Ranger had Tonto and a score of friends scattered across the terrain. The heroic, individualistic style of mission that some pastors seek to do is, finally, foolish. That is, it teaches people to live life in isolated and individualistic ways, whereas God calls us to live life in corporate community ways, in which, as we live out life's pilgrimage together, we do so with considerable sharing and caring, one with another.

The fourth invitational question about mission is, What events in the community would make this mission effort timely? It is interesting to me that a good many long-range planning committees do a sociological analysis of the community but fail to do a mission analysis of the community. Others have done more effective work in developing missions analysis. That is, rather than focusing on demographic data, they have focused thoughtfully on a study of the congregation, the groups within the congregation, the community, and the socioeconomic groupings within the community with a view to discovering (1) those major societal issues that are timely and pressing in the community, (2) those emerging groups likely to develop specific human hurts and hopes, and (3) the sense of the longings within given individuals and groups within the community at large to share concrete help.

To put that another way, events that occur in the church and community are among the final ingredients in developing missional objectives. The congregation or individuals within the congregation have sensed and been compelled by their own longings toward certain hurts and hopes. They have discovered strengths with which to respond. They have discovered one another as "mission teams." They have discovered that what they do now is timely. Events within the community have precipitated the kinds of quiet or dramatic crises that foster and nurture the congregation's compassionate response. This precipitating movement of community action, commensurate with the longings and strengths of given persons, invites the kind of dedicated and intentional missional outreach that has been effective throughout the history of the church.

The fifth invitational question is, In what specific ways is this emerging missional outreach one in which God is calling you to invest your life? Congregations and people who discover the joy of sharing effective mission do so because they commit their lives to a specific missional objective. They are not people who flit from one interest to another. To be sure, they share help as appropriate with whatever hurts and hopes come their way, but there is a kind of lifelong commitment to sharing effective help in a given area, one in which they feel God has called them to invest their lives.

I know of some congregations across this country who have invested years of courageous and effective help with alcoholics and their families. I know other congregations who have shared help with epileptics and their families. Others help those in the community who have experienced the death of a loved one or who have struggled with cancer. This list could go on and on. There is a sense in which congregations as well as individuals commit themselves to delivering effective help in a kind of lifelong pilgrimage to one or more specific, concrete, missional objectives to which they genuinely and authentically feel God has called them. The source of our longings to help is, finally, not our own petty interests or particular preferences. The longings to help have been placed within us by God, and, indeed, God uses his actions in the world to create precipitating events that call forth from us timely directions of effective help.

Living Legends of Help

Churches that share effective missional outreach with one or more specific human hurts or hopes become legends on the community grapevine. They become, in that community, the church that helps people with a given hurt and hope. They become the church that helped John and Mary. They become the church that helped Susie. They become a legend because they become participants in effective mission.

Regrettably, too many churches have developed the grapevine reputation of being interested in getting more members and more money so that they can do the maintenance things that need to be done with their buildings and programs. Regrettably, too many churches have become merry-go-rounds of programs and activities that focus on simplistic and petty understandings of life.

A church that genuinely and authentically becomes a church of the Good Shepherd develops, much to its surprise, a legendary character on the community grapevine. It becomes a church that is more interested in helping than being helped. It becomes a church that is more interested in loving than being loved. It becomes a church that is more interested in giving than in getting. It becomes one of the distinctive churches in the community—a church that gives itself away in effective missional service.

Ironically enough, people seek out churches who give themselves away. People stay away from churches whose only interest is self-interest. Those churches that are effectively in mission tend to be stable and growing congregations. This is not because their interest is in being stable and growing. No, it is because their interest is in sharing effective mission. When people have specific hurts and hopes, they are amazed and surprised to discover a congregation that is genuinely interested in being of help to them.

Rating Guide: Specific, Concrete Missional Objectives

Item	Maximum Points	Your Church's Rating
1. Does your church have one major mission delivering effective help and known and respected on the community grapevine?	40	_____
2. Is there another major mission delivering effective help and known and respected on the community grapevine?	30	_____
3. Is there a third major mission delivering effective help and known and respected on the community grapevine?	15	_____
4. Is there a major missional objective planned that will be brought on board by a specified date?	10	_____
5. Are there other missional objectives being considered for future implementation?	5	_____
Total:	100	_____

INSTRUCTIONS:
- Use the information in the chapter as a resource in evaluating your church's rating in each of the listed items.
- Enter the rating numbers in the blanks and then find the total.
- Divide the total of your assessment score by 10 to obtain your church's rating on a scale of 1 to 10.
- Enter the rating on the rating scale for Specific, Concrete Missional Objectives in Figure C.1.

2. Pastoral and Lay Visitation

$$\frac{30}{200} = 15\%$$

Visitation and Outreach

Generally speaking, a local congregation (with an average worship attendance of 200) has visitation and outreach well in place when the following is true:

3

1. The local congregation is sharing an average of twenty visits a week with its members and constituents.
2. The local congregation is sharing an average of twenty visits a week with unchurched persons in the community.
3. The local congregation is providing adequate visitation to persons who are hospitalized or homebound.

A congregation that is doing visitation minimally might be rated 1 or 2. A congregation that has focused its visitation primarily on members might rate its strength as 3, 4, or 5. The congregation that is focusing principally on members and newcomers might have a rating of 6 or 7. It is when the congregation focuses intentionally on visitation with members, constituents, newcomers, and unchurched—as well as sharing visitation with persons who are hospitalized or homebound—that that congregation has this foundational strength well in place and can rate itself as 8, 9, or 10.

In fact, the key to this characteristic is developing a balance of visitation with those who are participants (members and constituents) and those who are unchurched (those who have lived in the community a long time or those who are newcomers). The key to visitation is "to have one foot in the community and one foot in the church." That is, whenever the focus of visitation is within the church, one of the major sources of outreach in the community is lost. Whenever the visitation is primarily in the community, the strength of sharing and caring with those who are participants in the life and mission of the congregation is lost.

Overall, a good rule of thumb would be an average of twenty visits per week with participants in the church and twenty visits per week with people in the community (unchurched and newcomers) and adequate visitation to hospitals and homebound people. These visits would be made by the pastor and a range of key laypersons in the congregation. It would not be appropriate for the pastor to assume full responsibility for visitation; nor would it be appropriate for the pastor to train laypersons to do visitation and participate only minimally.

In smaller congregations (with an average worship attendance of 100) this number of visits could be appropriately reduced from twenty to ten or fifteen. By the same token, in larger congregations, the number of visits shared per week would increase proportionately. For example, a congregation of 3,000 members plus 2,000 constituents and approximately 1,500 persons who are being served in missional ways in the community would want to substantially increase the number of visits it makes per week in order to be able to rate itself 8, 9, or 10.

Over the years, numerous pastors have asked my thoughts as to what constitutes an adequate range of visitation for the pastor. Basically, I have suggested the following rule of thumb; in some circles it has become known as Callahan's Principle of Visitation: Spend one hour in pastoral visitation each week for every minute you preach on Sunday morning. That is, it will be helpful toward the development of an effective and successful church for the pastor who preaches twenty minutes on Sunday morning to share approximately twenty hours per week in visitation with members, constituents, newcomers, unchurched, and hospitalized and homebound persons. This rule of thumb invites pastors to develop skills in time management. Further, it invites pastors to think through those strategic priorities that will best advance a church toward becoming increasingly effective and successful.

Clearly, specific, concrete missional objectives and adequate pastoral and lay visitation are the two central characteristics with which a local congregation increases its capacity to reach out into the community. If a local church could have only two of the twelve strengths so well in place as to be rated 8, 9, or 10, it would be important for mission and visitation to be the two. It is not accidental that they are number 1 and number 2 among the twelve. Without these two responsibly in place, there is a strong likelihood that a church would be either stable and declining or dying. These two strengths are the two that enable the church to most effectively reach the unchurched persons within the local community.

Mission Visitation

Visitation Analysis

Since it is so important, it is helpful for the local congregation to do an analysis of precisely where it is investing its time in pastoral and lay visitation. This is particularly important because, among many churches across the country, there is preoccupation with visiting newcomers in the community and only token efforts to visit members. Regrettably, in many churches, there is hardly any focus on visitation with unchurched persons or with constituents in the local congregation. This preoccupation with newcomers is insidious. It simply ignores vast numbers of unchurched persons who have been living within average driving time of that congregation for years—and who do not participate in the life and mission of any congregation in the community.

Visitation analysis can also help a congregation think through the appropriate balance between pastoral and lay visits. It is a sad commentary that a number of ministers have the notion that it is their responsibility to train the laity to do the visitation so that the laity can go out in the world to visit. Such pastors do not see themselves as being substantively involved in visitation. The best that can be said for them is that they are naive.

That is, it is incongruous for a person to say "I will train you to do visitation. That's the responsibility of the pastor, but you are the people who should do the visitation." The most effective visitation programs I have seen across the country have been effective precisely because the pastor has taken a major role in actually doing visitation. The pastor has been in the lead. This is extraordinarily helpful, because the pastor who does regular visitation teaches the congregation, both directly and indirectly, the value of this activity in the life and mission of the congregation. The visitation analysis chart in Figure 2.1 will give you the opportunity to think through where your church stands on this strength.

Figure 2.1   Visitation Analysis Chart

Frequently, an effective local church makes an average of 40 visits per week, approximately 20 with members and constituents and 20 with unchurched and newcomer families.

Please indicate pastoral and lay visits separately, then total for both.

1. Number of visits in average week with members

Pastoral visits _____

Lay visits _____

Total _____

2. Number of visits in average week with constituents

Pastoral visits _____

Lay visits _____

Total _____

3. Number of visits in average week with unchurched in the community

Pastoral visits _____

Lay visits _____

Total _____

4. Number of visits in average week with newcomers

Pastoral visits _____

Lay visits _____

Total _____

Visitation-Mission-Growth

There is a direct correlation between visitation, mission, and church growth. Indeed, it has been my experience that those churches who substantially engage in visitation and mission are precisely those churches that have the best possibility for growth. The material that follows identifies the steps of a basic formula (Figure 2.2) with which a

---

Figure 2.2   Visitation-Mission-Growth Formula

1. Determine the number of visits per week to be shared with unchurched families and newcomer families.

    For example, it is reasonable for a medium-to-large church to share 20 such visits per week. The pastor might make 10 of these visits and a lay visitation committee might accomplish 10 of these visits.

    Number planned per week   _____

2. Determine the number of mission visits to be shared per year with un-churched families and newcomer families by multiplying the number of visits per week (from step 1) by the number of weeks per year that visits are made.

    For example, multiply the 20 visits per week by 48 weeks (the number of weeks the pastor and lay visitation committee intentionally work at visitation) to arrive at 960 visits per year.

    Number planned per year   _____

3. Divide the total number of visits per year (from step 2) by the average number of visits per family that will be shared during that year.

    There is considerable evidence to suggest that an average of 5 visits per family is necessary to effectively minister to and/or reach that family. In our example, therefore, this would mean that 192 families per year would benefit from the mission of the local church.

    Families visited per year   _____

4. Calculate the percentage of families that will become active in the church as constituents and/or members by taking 20–33% of families visited per year (from step 3).

    It is reasonable to estimate that 20–33% of the total unchurched families and newcomer families that are visited intentionally in a given year will become active participants in that local church. In our example, it means that 38 to 63 of the 192 families are likely to become participants in that local church.

    Projected increase in participants   _____

---

church can predict the range of participants it is likely to receive as the result of a consequential focus on visitation with unchurched persons. This formula has been tested over the past decade with many churches. Again and again, it has proven accurate as a conservative predictor of church growth.

It is important to realize that the purpose of these visits with unchurched families is not to get them into the church. I would describe these as mission visits where the focus is on sharing effective help and resources with unchurched persons as they seek to live meaningfully and fully in everyday life. Indeed, the focus is on being the church with them where they are rather than on seeking to get them to come to church on Sunday morning. This self-giving approach is the most responsible form of mission visitation.

It is my experience that it takes approximately five to nine visits to share effectively in mission with unchurched persons. Regrettably, there are many visitation workshops that suggest to people that the objectives of visitation can be accomplished in one or two visits. This is hustling more than it is helping. It constitutes a focus on what the person visiting can get done quickly. It focuses more on what we want to get from the person being visited than on what we want to share with them.

Four *Major Stages of Visitation*

You may find it helpful to think of four major stages of visitation. The first is selecting and seeking. Even given the vast number of unchurched persons in our culture, there is an even greater number of church people who have not had a visit in their home from a pastor or layperson on behalf of the church in a decade or more. It is therefore important for those leaders who plan to engage in visitation to select intentionally and thoughtfully the persons whom they plan to visit during the coming year. This focus on visitation should be intentional and active rather than haphazard and responsive. The first step is to thoughtfully select the persons to be visited and to seek them out in their homes, places of work, or places of recreation. It is not likely these persons will seek us out. It is far more likely that either we will seek them out or nothing in the way of mission and sharing will take place. Perhaps the hardest of the four stages is selecting the persons to be visited and seeking them out. It invites pastors to leave the safety of their offices and the pleasantness of their committee meetings to be active courageously in the world.

2. The second major stage is sharing and shepherding. In this stage, the person who is visiting shares mutually and creatively with the person being visited. They come to know one another as individuals. They come to know something of one another's mutual strengths, hurts, and hopes.

They begin to develop a sense of shepherding, that is, caring. The pastor or layperson doing visitation would seek to do other than "pastoral counseling." The reason I prefer the term "shepherding" is that it is a more encompassing term. It describes the range and variety of ways in which people mutually help one another.

3. The third major stage of visitation is relating and reaching. That is, the visitor seeks to relate to this individual or family at a deeper level than simply that of pleasant acquaintance and to reach out to them on behalf of Christ. This reaching out takes the form of inviting them to accept Christ and become participants in the life and mission of the Christian church. It does not take the form of reaching out to invite them to join in a pleasant merry-go-round of programs that go on within the safety and confines of a local church. That is too superficial. The deepest and most responsible form of reaching out is to share invitationally with them in their lives and to reach out to them that they might decide to become participants in the life and, particularly, the mission of the Christian church.

4. The fourth stage is winning and working. Finally, it is God who wins persons to His kingdom and to His cause, not us. And these persons whom God has won, just as He has won us, become involved in working on behalf of reconciliation, wholeness, caring, and justice in the world, not simply in the church. The working is a working in God's kingdom, not in the local church's cultural programs and activities. These frequently inoculate people into a superficial safety, and thereby, they avoid the deep hurts and hopes that are present in the world.

The Major Stages of Visitation chart (Figure 2.3) enables the congregation to do an analysis of the range of groups with which they are engaged in visitation. The chart invites the local congregation to think through which of the four major stages of visitation they have achieved with people in each group.

It is easier to learn an active and intentional approach to visitation that focuses on human hurts and hopes if one visits initially the first five groups on the chart. These five groups have some things in common with us missionally, relationally, and sociologically but do not have in common present participation in our church. The danger in visitation with the other groups is that too much time may be spent focusing on conversation about the church and not enough time focusing on the hurts and hopes that we share.

The art of visitation is a developmental art. One does it best when one does it regularly. One does it best when one does it over a period of years. It is not an art one learns quickly or easily, because it is finally the art of responsibly helping people with their human hurts and hopes in an active, intentional, seeking-out way.

Development Possibilities

Whom to Select

Five factors are worth consideration as a local church selects those individuals whom they plan to visit intentionally during the coming year:

1. Mission. Select those households wherein—insofar as it is possible to know—there are human hurts and hopes in everyday life that are commensurate with the specific, concrete missional objectives toward which the church is working.

2. Relational Neighborhood. People live in three kinds of neighborhoods. They live in a relational neighborhood of friends, kin, business associates, and close acquaintances. People also live in a socioeconomic-cultural neighborhood and in a geographical neighborhood. The most effective neighborhood is the relational neighborhood, and the art of visitation has something to do with tracking the network of relationships people share with one another across the community.

3. Like Us or Nearly Like Us. This is a socioeconomic-cultural neighborhood. It is important to note that on the chart the first area to consider is mission and only the third area to consider is the principle of homogeneity.

4. Travel Direction Pattern. As has been observed earlier, people tend to drive to church in approximately the same direction that they drive to work, to do major shopping, and to participate in major social and recreational activities. It will take possibly five visits to reach a household where the traffic direction pattern and the location of the church are compatible. It may take nine or more visits to reach a household if you are inviting them to go to church in a direction different from their normal traffic direction pattern. That is not to say that one should give up or not seek out those who live in a divergent traffic direction pattern; rather, it is to affirm that they are likely to require a larger investment in mission visitation.

5. Average Travel Time. It will be easier to be in mission with those persons whose average trip time in day-to-day life and average trip time in relation to the church are compatible.

It would be my suggestion that the first households the local church selects to visit should fit three out of five of the above-mentioned criteria, if at all possible. The reason for this is to assure a better chance of being effective and successful in mission visitation at the outset. This will prevent the visitors from becoming discouraged and giving up. Later, when that local congregation is more substantially confident of their

Figure 2.3 Analysis of Major Stages of Visitation

	Selecting and Seeking	Sharing and Shepherding	Relating and Reaching	Winning and Working
Persons Served in Mission (unchurched)				
Friends and Kin (unchurched)				
Like Us (unchurched, in same socioeconomic category, within our average trip time)				
Nearly Like Us (unchurched, in similar socioeconomic category, within our average trip time)				
Newcomers				

Church Visitors				
Constituents				
Sunday School Visitors				
Shut-ins				
Active Members				
Marginally Active Members				
Inactive Members				

In each box, indicate the number of households with which your church is presently in visitation. It is important to try to be accurate about which stage your visitation with a particular household has reached.

competency to do mission visitation, it will be able to visit people across the community whose "profile" may be quite distinct from any of the five criteria mentioned above.

Five Steps in a Visit

It would be worth noting here the five basic steps in effective visitation and following some of the basic principles.

1. First Statement. The opening statement the visitor shares with the person being visited establishes the direction, the content, and the limits of the visit. Too many people in their first statement use an innocuous throwaway line. It is far more instructive to set forth honestly and thoughtfully the central objective for one's visiting in that household.

2. The First Three Minutes. The initial objective, direction, content, and limits of the visit are reconfirmed and put solidly in place during the first three minutes, or the person being visited will develop the impression that the visitor is someone who does not know why he or she has come.

3. Development of Mutual Objectives. In each visit it is important that both the person visiting and the person being visited discover and share mutual objectives that deepen the character and quality of the relationship that they are in the process of developing.

4. Closing. The closing of the visit is simply and straightforwardly shared. Avoid closing a visit in an awkward or artificial way. Generally speaking, it is helpful to begin closing the visit within fifteen or twenty minutes of having come.

5. Leaving. When leaving, it is important to leave well and to leave in such fashion that both parties look forward with some modest anticipation to that time when they might have the privilege of sharing and visiting with each other again.

Ten Foundational Principles of the Art of Effective Visitation

1. Decide on one to three key objectives that you hope to accomplish in this specific visit.
2. Decide the exact time you plan to leave. Don't stay too long.
3. Share in prayer with God *before* you ring the doorbell. Perhaps your prayer will ask that God help you to listen to what is being said, to listen beneath what is being said, and to listen for what is not said, so you can be genuinely helpful in a mutual way with this person.
4. Dress in such a fashion that you communicate that you have the capacity to be a source of stability and reliability—a source of help

and hope. Such dress will vary from one part of the country to another. Certainly it is not my intent to prescribe what to wear—it is simply to affirm that people form their impressions of who the visitor is both by what the visitor says and by what the visitor looks like. You can never make a first impression the second time.

5. Stand in a nonthreatening position as you ring the doorbell. Do not stand in an aggressive, forward stance that suggests intrusion. Rather, stand, generally speaking, to the side of the door so that those who answer the door will see that you don't intend to intrude on their space.

6. Begin the visit with who they are. Do not begin the visit with yourself.

7. Focus on the relational dynamics of life, not the functional dynamics. Should questions be asked about the church, share with them the relational strengths (significant relational groups, corporate dynamic worship) that are present in your church, not the functional strengths (adequate parking, adequate space and facilities). They will be more interested in the relational ones.

8. During the course of the visit, share with them in mutual ways. Avoid asking more than two or three questions in the whole visit. The purpose of the visit is not an interrogation to discover information. The purpose of the visit is to establish the beginnings of a relationship. Therefore, the focus of the visit must be mutual, not a one-way series of questions and answers.

9. Leave while the visit is still on an upswing, don't wait until it has started downhill. There are two reasons for this. First, whatever level you leave a given visit, you will pick up at that same point when next you visit. It is much easier in the next visit to pick it up at a point where the visit had already been going up. It is much harder to pick it up when the previous visit had been going downhill. The second reason is that some of the deeper sharing of hurts and hopes occurs as the visitor is moving to the door. It is important to move to the door soon enough so that that process can occur. If the visitor stays an hour and then moves to the door, people will simply be glad the visitor is gone.

10. End the visit by focusing on them, not giving an excuse for leaving. Do not say, "Yes I had better be going. I have a meeting at the church." It would be much more helpful to say, "John and Mary, I have enjoyed our visit together. I look forward to the possibility of our visiting again in the near future. It's been good to be with you. Good-bye."

~~Three~~ Key Strengths for Effective Visitation

There are no gimmicks. There are three key strengths that many people already have that will enable them to be constructively effective in visitation. The first is their capacity to share friendships. The best skill most people have for doing visitation is their skill in developing friendships. This is not to say that the focus of visitation is simply to develop friendships. Rather, it is to say that at least the beginnings of a friendship are important as one seeks to be in a sharing and shepherding mission with another person.

The second key strength is the longing to help with specific human hurts and hopes. Once individuals have discovered and claimed their own individual longings they are in a strong position to discover ways to fulfill their helping mission with people in the surrounding community.

The third key strength has to do with the hope and vision for the future that people have. Those people who have a confident and powerful sense of hope and whose vision of the future is solid and strong are more likely to have the competence and confidence to share deeply and fully with others in mission visitation. These are the ones who are most likely to have the strength to deal with the pain and suffering, the hurts and hopes, that they will discover in visitation.

Sharing and Caring

Life is a pilgrimage. One of the rare gifts of our pilgrimage on this planet is the discovery of people with whom we can develop sharing and caring relationships. Pastoral and lay visitation provides one major avenue through which people can seek out their fellow human beings and begin to develop the sense of common pilgrimage, one with another.

The purpose of pastoral and lay visitation is not to hustle people into the neat and nifty programs and activities of a local church. The purpose of pastoral and lay visitation is a deeper, more profound discovery of central and common relationships among fellow travelers through this life's journey. A decisive advantage of the church putting well in place the central characteristic of pastoral and lay visitation is that amazingly enough the congregation will discover the richness of relationships with people who strengthen and develop their own capacities and competencies to help and to be helped.

Rating Guide: Pastoral and Lay Visitation

Item	Maximum Points	Your Church's Rating
1. Does your church have an adequate program of visitation of members and constituents?	25	_____
2. Adequate visitation of unchurched and newcomers?	25	_____
3. Adequate visitation in hospitals, nursing homes and with the homebound?	25	_____
4. How high is the quality of sharing and shepherding?	25	_____
Total:	100	_____

INSTRUCTIONS:

- Use the information in the chapter as a resource in evaluating your church's rating in each of the listed items.
- Enter the rating numbers in the blanks and then find the total.
- Divide the total of your assessment score by 10 to obtain your church's rating on a scale of 1 to 10.
- Enter that rating on the rating scale for Pastoral and Lay visitation in Figure C.1.

3. Corporate, Dynamic Worship

Worship and the Unchurched

Corporate, dynamic worship is the third central characteristic found in most effective and successful congregations. Worship is extraordinarily important in the unchurched culture in which we are engaged in mission. That is, it is highly likely that many of the unchurched persons whom a church reaches in mission or visitation will find their way first to the service of worship. In the 1950s and early 1960s, it was frequently the case that unchurched persons found their way into the life and mission of the local congregation through a small group. Indeed, much emphasis was placed upon this. This still occurs, but now more often unchurched persons find their way first to the service of worship. Thus, corporate, dynamic worship becomes an increasingly important avenue through which people are reached on behalf of Christ.

Worship is corporate whenever there is a strong sense of belonging, a strong sense of togetherness and community, among the people who share in it. Worship is dynamic whenever the service stirs and inspires the people who participate in it and whenever profound help and hope are shared with and among them. Worship does not need to be fancy or complex. Nor does it need to contain gimmicks and razzle-dazzle. Rather, it means that people experience their togetherness in a simple, profound way amidst the dynamic gospel that shares with them help and hope.

Five factors contribute to corporate, dynamic worship. It will be helpful for the reader to evaluate a given service of worship in relation to each of the five and to do so as accurately and as honestly as possible. Generally speaking, whenever four or five of these factors are strongly present, then worship is corporate and dynamic enough to rate 8, 9, or 10 on our scale of 1 to 10. Whenever two or three of these factors are present, worship is correspondingly a 4, 5, or 6 on a scale of 1 to 10.

Detailed Specifications

The Warmth and Winsomeness of the Service and the Congregation

The sense of warmth and winsomeness is the first thing to be discerned as one studies the ways in which members and constituents relate one to another before, during, and after the service of worship. Do members of the congregation have a sense of grace? Do they operate from a theology of love? Do the people in the church evidence that they are the body of Christ in community one with another? Do the people who are members and constituents share a fellowship as Christian friends—a fellowship that shares with them strength and help and hope?

These are pointed questions, but they are not meant to be used as instruments of church masochism or self-criticism. Rather, these questions can be used as a means of evaluating the quality of warmth that members and constituents share one with another and to obtain a firm grasp of the climate of caring and sharing present among those who participate in worship together. In churches where people experience this depth of warmth, worshipers generally leave a service surprised and profoundly grateful for the time they have shared one with another. They feel as though they have been helped because they have joined hands with their fellows in Christ, and they feel as though they have received a sense of confident hope with which to live out everday life.

The sense of warmth can be further discerned as one studies ways in which a local congregation provides for and interacts with visitors who worship with their congregation. Does the sense of grace and community that church members share with each other also find its way genuinely and authentically to visitors? Visitors do not come to church by accident. They do not come simply because they are shopping around for a church home. They come looking for that sense of fellowship, encouragement, help, and hope. They come for community, not so they will be put on a committee.

The impression that visitors have of the warmth of a church will hinge primarily on the experiences they have as they interact with parking supervisors, greeters, ushers, leaders of the service of worship, and those who are seated around them. Frequently, the first person a visitor will meet at a large church is a parking supervisor. Thus, for such a church to make a good first impression as a warm congregation, the parking supervisor must be something more than a traffic direction officer. Parking supervisors should appropriately convey a sense of warmth and joy in their task, give competent, clearly understood instructions about parking possibilities, and provide extra attention to those with special needs, such as handicapped persons, for example. If your church wants to make the right first impression, those who supervise the parking must be chosen carefully.

The same is true of leaders and ushers. In most churches that share corporate, dynamic worship in strong ways, there are two kinds of greeters. First, there are those greeters who stand at the doors of the church and greet everyone—that is, members, constituents, and visitors. Second, there are those who have been asked to serve as "new-person greeters."

The same people should serve as "new-person greeters" each week. It is not best for this group of individuals to alternate weekly or monthly. Indeed, they must be the people who know the congregation so well that they will know when someone is new. Their ministry, then, is to welcome the new persons who come to that service of worship. The new-person greeters are warm, sincere, and thoughtfully friendly individuals. They have a natural ability to help people to feel at home. Generally, they have some capacity to remember names. Frequently, when a new-person greeter welcomes by name visitors who come for the second time—even if that second time is three weeks later than their first visit—from that point on those visitors begin to think of that church as their home church, because someone knows them by name and that person cares for them in simple ways.

Ushers are also an important dimension in communicating the corporate and dynamic character of a service of worship. As with greeters, it is helpful for the ushers to have a sincere spirit of warmth and tenderness. They do not simply hand out bulletins or name tags; they work closely with the new-person greeters. When new people visit a given church, it is important the ushers seat them next to people who are somewhat like them. For example, if the visitors are a young couple with children, it makes sense to seat them in that section of the congregation where young couples customarily sit. If the visitors are two older widows, it may make good sense to seat them where several older widows normally sit. As people are seated and they look around them, they make some decision about whether there are people who are reasonably like them in this church or not. The older couple seated among very young couples may feel out of place, as might the young couple seated among older people, even though in the congregation as a whole there may be more people like them than are seated around them. The basic point is that people evaluate how well they fit in based on who they see sitting around them on their first visit.

There is a sense, therefore, in which the entire progression—from the car to the parking lot, to the narthex, to the pew—should have the character of warmth about it in which friendship, in the best sense of the term, has been experienced and expressed. Throughout this progression, visitors should be greeted in love and warmth. They should be made to feel welcome, to sense that they are appreciated as distinctive human beings, not as numbers to add to the attendance figures. They must know that they have found a place where Christ's words of hope and resurrection have become real.

A further source of warmth and winsomeness is the leaders of the service of worship. More often than not, they share this sense of warmth implicitly, not explicitly. I have been in churches where the words spoken were words of love, warmth, and caring, but the tone implied judgment, legalism, and law. Likewise, I have been in other churches where a sense of forgiveness, reconciliation, grace, and hope are implicit. Indeed, this has more to do with the manner in which the service is led than it does with the order of service itself. The more the service is led out of a theology of grace the more likely the members, constituents, and visitors will experience that service of worship as sharing warmth and winsomeness.

The Dynamic and Inspiration of the Music

Music constitutes 40 percent of the service of worship. On those Sundays when my own preaching is off, I count on the music to carry the service. Music is extraordinarily important in the course of the worship service, and a solid music program is vital to achieve corporate, dynamic worship. A strong music program generally has three ingredients: planning and spontaneity, balance and variety, and quality and depth.

Planning and spontaneity in all components of the worship service are important. The service cannot have unity and direction unless those who lead the service of worship share in the planning. It is equally important that those who lead music, those who lead liturgy, and those who preach have sufficient trust and respect for one another and for the quality of teamwork they share that they can move with spontaneity as a team when the Spirit leads them in a new direction during the course of the worship service. Improvisation and spontaneity build on the planning that has already occurred. The worship leaders need to have the sense of trust and cooperation of a drama repertory company or a great jazz ensemble, or that of a basketball team that has played well together and almost knows where one another are on the court without even looking.

The second ingredient is the sense of balance and variety that the music provides in the service of worship. If one were to draw a line and on one end of the line put the words "simple," "profound," and "emotional" and on the other end of the line put the words "complex," "comprehensive," and "intellectual," the music and the preaching should be balanced between them. This does not necessarily mean that the music is a variety of Ralph Vaughan Williams one week and Bill Gaither the next. If the preaching tends to be complex, comprehensive, and intellectual, then it becomes important that the music be simple, profound, and emotional so that a wider range of the spectrum is covered during the course of the worship service. That is what is meant by the sense of balance and variety. It is difficult to obtain but most important to the worship service.

The third ingredient is the quality and depth of the music itself. The work of the pianist, the organist, the choir director, and the choir itself should be of high quality. It is important that the music be played and sung competently and that the people who sing it be committed Christians. Their commitment as Christians will not compensate for a lack of competence. Indeed, it is precisely their commitment that fuels their desire to be one of the best choirs to the glory of God in the community that surrounds the church.

The Character and Quality of the Preaching

The whole service has to do with the gospel, which is good news. Some preachers have a tendency to forget this foundational conviction of the Christian faith, namely, that the gospel is good news. Too often I have found preachers turning grace into law, good news into judgment, and love into legalism.

It is clearly the case that judgment, sin, and law have an appropriate place in the Christian faith. It is the case that Jesus intensified rather than eased many of the human tensions among us. One of those tensions is the constant struggle between law and gospel, demand and grace. Clearly, the law is in the biblical message; sin, demand, judgment, are indeed New Testament themes. The parables of Jesus do speak of outer darkness and the weeping and gnashing of teeth.

The preacher who dwells week after week on judgment, sin, and law as the Bible's primary themes is telling only part of the message. Law is strong, grace is stronger. Christians, both clergy and laity, must grasp once again the ringing message of the New Testament that hope is stronger than memory, that the open tomb is stronger than the bloody cross, that the risen Lord is stronger than the dead Jesus. God loves us.

It is this message that people need to hear. People come to church to be helped, to be loved. They come to church to be comforted and to be challenged. Sometimes the help people *need* is not the help that they *want*. But what people come searching for is help and hope that they might live everyday life more fully and richly. It is difficult to live through a week in a world full of hatred, violence, disappointment, and despair. It is difficult to live through a week if the preaching that is shared is primarily a manifestation of that same hatred, violence, disappointment, and despair. People are helped when the preaching leads them to the spirit of reconciliation, caring, and justice that is a persistent theme in the New Testament message.

It is important that the quality of preaching be that of love and grace and that the character of the preaching have sufficient backbone to share that in genuinely helpful ways.

Preachers who share corporate, dynamic sermons have three things in common. First, their sermons are easily followed and they make sense. Second, their sermons involve the humor, struggle, and drama of the biblical text and of contemporary living. Third, their sermons share something with the congregation that is hopeful and helpful in the midst of the pain, suffering, and injustice present in the world.

The great preachers of our time are generally found in small and medium-sized churches. These are the preachers who are the shepherds, leaders, and prophets in their churches and community. They have been shepherds in their caring and sharing. They have become leaders with their wisdom and judgment. They have become prophets with their thoughtful and insightful critique that advances help and hope in our society.

The Power and Movement of the Liturgy

Worship services that have a sense of power and movement in the liturgy are those in which the service is a unified whole. The preceding stages build toward and contribute to the next stage in the service, and there is a sense of progression and movement toward the climax of moving into the world in mission as God's people.

Some services of worship are simply a series of disconnected stages that occur one after another. There is no sense of development and progression. There is no sense of growth and power, no sense of movement and direction.

This is not to speak in favor of either high church or low church liturgy. One can find power and movement in both. One can also find a sense of disconnectedness and lack of direction in both low church and high church liturgy. It is decisive that the liturgy share something of the power and movement of the gospel and the rhythms that move toward new life in Christ.

The Seating Range of the Sanctuary

The impact of the physical space in which worship takes place should be given consideration at this point. I am addressing the *perceptions* the worshiper has in response to the surroundings during the worship service. Generally speaking, the experience of corporate and dynamic worship takes place in sanctuaries that are comfortably filled.

With respect to the perceptions of space, there are four types of sanctuaries: uncomfortably crowded, comfortably filled, comfortably empty, and uncomfortably empty. Several factors contribute to a sanctuary being perceived in the comfortable seating ranges: a wide center aisle or aisles, wide side aisles, a large vestibule, short pews, and a spacious chancel at the front of the sanctuary.

Wide aisles obviously contribute to the ease of entering and leaving the sanctuary. Additionally, the roominess they provide allows freedom to stop and greet someone as you pass without obstructing others as they move to find their seats. The visiting and fellowship before and after the worship service enhances the sense of togetherness and community.

A large vestibule further contributes to the possibility of establishing relationships through visiting, sharing, and caring. Importantly, the large vestibule gives worshipers a strong sense of spaciousness.

Short pews, seating up to eight people, are more desirable than longer pews in a sanctuary. Many people even arrive early in hopes of finding available aisle seating. Some people will step past those on the aisle to sit somewhat more toward the middle of the pew, but generally people don't like to feel "trapped" in the middle. Visitors are particularly sensitive to claustrophobic seating.

The chancel area is another significant factor in the sense of spaciousness in the sanctuary as a whole. The more spacious and open the chancel area is, the more likely people are to feel comfortable in their seating, even if they are in fact somewhat crowded. In a comfortably filled sanctuary, a cluttered and crowded chancel causes the sanctuary to be perceived as uncomfortably crowded.

Most people prefer to worship in a sanctuary that is comfortably filled. Next, people prefer a sanctuary that is comfortably empty. Then, people prefer a sanctuary that is uncomfortably empty. Last of all will people be willing to put up with worshiping in a sanctuary that is uncomfortably crowded. They will do so mainly on Christmas and Easter because that is to be expected. From Sunday to Sunday people prefer not to worship in a sanctuary that is uncomfortably crowded.

A church that has an uncomfortably crowded sanctuary would be wise to add another service or expand the size of the sanctuary—or consider building a new sanctuary. Those churches that are able to get away with having an uncomfortably crowded sanctuary from Sunday to Sunday, year in and year out, are those churches that deliver extraordinarily solid preaching, great music, and/or strong pastoral visitation throughout the week. Without those three factors well in place—along with a substantial number of significant relational groups—it is generally not possible for a church to sustain an uncomfortably crowded worship attendance Sunday after Sunday—unless they are simply turning over a lot of vistors each Sunday.

The chart in Figure 3.1 will enable you to ascertain the maximum "comfortably filled" seating capacity of your sanctuary. It should be pointed out that most sanctuaries in cities and small towns become comfortably filled at approximately 80 percent of total seating capacity. Rural sanctuaries in town and country settings tend to become comfortably filled at 50 to 70 percent of total seating capacity. People who

Figure 3.1   Maximum "Comfortably Filled" Seating Capacity Formula

There are four kinds of sanctuaries: uncomfortably crowded, comfortably filled, comfortably empty, and uncomfortably empty. Work through this formula to determine the "comfortably filled" seating capacity of your sanctuary.

1. Main floor seating capacity
   (Omit front pew unless a railing is present.)   _____
2. Choir seating capacity   _____
3. Adjusted balcony seating
   (Take 50% of total balcony seating.)   _____
4. Adjusted overflow and transept seating (Transept
   side room in cross-shaped church, or back room in
   rectangular church: Take 50–75% of overflow and
   transept seating, depending on lines of sight)   _____
5. Total gross seating capacity (add 1–4)   _____
6. Comfortably filled with
   a. wide center aisle (or double aisles)
   b. wide side aisles
   c. large vestibule
   d. short pews (seating 8 or fewer)
   e. spacious chancel   _____
   is 80% of total gross seating capacity in cities and
   towns, 60% in rural areas.
7. Adjusted comfortably filled figure
   (Reduce by approximately 4% each for the lack of
   any of the characteristics *a–e* mentioned in 6 above.)   _____

have chosen to have substantial elbow room in everyday life—living on farms five to ten acres apart—tend to want a stronger sense of spaciousness in their sanctuary than people who live in urban apartments and homes.

Development Possibilities

About developing the service of worship so that it becomes corporate and dynamic, three observations should be made. The first is about the pastor: The more fully the pastor is shepherd, leader, and preacher, the more likely the service of worship will be corporate and dynamic. It should be noted that the order is (1) shepherd, (2) leader, and (3) preacher. Regrettably, too many pastors go to a church planning to be great preachers before they have become caring shepherds. Their cart is in front of their horse.

The point can be made this way: Two pastors both rank at about 7 on a scale of 1 to 10 in preaching. One is a shepherd and leader, as well as a preacher. The other is neither shepherd nor leader. The leader-shepherd preacher will be perceived by his congregation as preaching at a level of 8 or 9. The other pastor—neither shepherd nor leader—will be perceived as preaching at a level of 5 or 6.

Two factors contribute to this dynamic. First, the pastor who in caring, loving ways knows the people as a good shepherd and a solid leader is able to preach richly and fully to their hurts and hopes in ordinary everyday life. A pastor who has not taken the time to be a shepherd with them will not know what these specific hurts and hopes are and can only preach generalized, innocuous sermons. Second, when the people know that the pastor knows them, cares for them, and loves them, they therefore listen more respectfully and attentively. They will listen to those who will share the gospel in their life as well as their message, in their mission as well as their words.

The second observation about developing the service of worship has to do with the staff person in music. It is my recommendation that, whether part-time or full-time, the second key staff person a local church employs be someone gifted and competent in the field of music. In most instances, this is likely to be a part-time person initially. The resources that a gifted and competent director of music can bring to the service of worship are extraordinary. Across the country in small churches I have seen both volunteer and paid staff people serving as directors of music bring an amazing richness to the dynamic and inspiration of the service.

Thirdly, it is worth noting that there is a direct correlation between worship attendance and membership growth and income. Those churches that have increased their worship attendance tend also to discover that their membership grows and their financial resources increase as well. Frankly, those churches whose primary objectives are increasing their membership and improving their giving are working on the wrong strategic objectives. As a matter of fact, they would do better to work on the objective of increasing worship attendance. The by-products of that alone would be an increase in membership and an increase in giving.

It is well to observe that increases in both membership and giving *are* by-products, not ends in themselves. We do not work to increase worship attendance as a means to the ends of more members and more giving. Rather, we genuinely and thoughtfully share corporate, dynamic worship in outreaching and outgoing ways for the help and hope it delivers in people's lives. This self-giving approach to the service of worship may very likely result in an increase in membership and an increase in giving, but those potential results should not be seen as the primary purposes for developing corporate and dynamic worship.

Conclusion

In recent years, so much attention has been given to the development of small groups within the congregation that worship has become a neglected component in the life of many congregations. To be sure, pastors discuss among themselves the old axiom of spending one hour in preparation for each minute of preaching. The truth of the matter is that very little planning goes into many services of worship. Further, even pastors who do spend substantial amounts of time in preparing their sermons do so out of a model of writing sermons to be read rather than developing sermons to be heard and received.

Effective, successful congregations invest an appropriate amount of time and leadership in developing services of worship that are corporate and dynamic. Frequently, this means having strong music resources. Frequently, it means having pastors who prepare their preaching as they care for their people as much as they prepare it in the safety and quiet of a study. Worship will continue in the forseeable future to be one of the major places where unchurched persons and newcomers come to discover whether a congregation will share with them help and hope in strong, warm and winsome ways.

Rating Guide: Corporate, Dynamic Worship

Item	Maximum Points	Your Church's Rating
1. What is the degree of warmth and winsomeness both of the service and of the congregation?	20	_____
2. How dynamic and inspirational is the music?	25	_____
3. Does the character and quality of the preaching come from the pastor's care as a good shepherd?	25	_____
4. Is there strong progression in the power and movement of the liturgy?	10	_____
5. How adequate is the seating in the sanctuary?	20	_____
Total:	100	_____

INSTRUCTIONS:

- Use the information in the chapter as a resource in evaluating your church's rating in each of the listed items.
- Enter the rating numbers in the blanks and then find the total.
- Divide the total of your assessment score by 10 to obtain your church's rating on a scale of 1 to 10.
- Enter that rating on the rating scale for Corporate, Dynamic Worship in Figure C.1.

4. Significant Relational Groups

Community, Not Committees

People search for community, not for committees. People will put up with being on committees to the extent that they have discovered community. Frequently, the most lively times are before and after the committee meeting as people stand around and share with one another the sense of community.

Most people have four life searches: for individuality, community, meaning, and hope. The search for individuality is the search for integrity and power in one's existence and destiny. The search for meaning is the search for the discovery of purpose and values in ordinary everyday life. The search for hope is the search for a reliable and certain future.

The search for community is the search for roots, place, and belonging—for a group of people in which significant relationships of sharing and caring can take place. We are who we are as a result of the groups that have informed and enriched our own sense of individuality, of meaning and purpose in life, and of hope for the future. Most people engage in a persistent search for the kind of community that will enrich their lives and enable them to discover and fulfill these four life searches in that covenant community.

Indeed, effective, successful congregations share a strong theology of community and provide substantial relationships of sharing and caring in the various groups constituting that particular church. Wherever the covenant of reconciliation, wholeness, caring, and justice takes place, there one discovers community. Wherever proleptic experiences of the kingdom occur, wherever events of mission are shared, wherever people live life's pilgrimage with each other and for the world, there one discovers community.

People are not simply searching for contracts; they are searching for covenant. They are not searching for programs and activities or institutional structures, but for proleptic experiences of kingdom and events of mission in which they can share. They are not searching for a merry-go-round of business activities and committee meetings; they are searching for people with whom they can live out life together.

New People and New Groups

More often than not, new people will first find their way to a church in response to the mission or visitation outreach of that congregation. Frequently, the first place they will "touch base" with that congregation is in the service of worship. Insofar as they find the service of worship corporate and dynamic, they will begin to look around for a group with whom they can share significant relationships of sharing and caring. Some people may begin the process of looking for a significant relational group having visited the service of worship as few as three or four times.

More often than not, people wait much longer than that before they search with any intensity for such a group. Generally speaking, within the first six months, and in some instances within the first year and a half, people will need to discover such a group or they will be likely to join that great Sunday school class in the sky called inactive members. One of the key factors that increases newcomers' interest in the life and mission of a congregation is their ability to find a sense of roots, place, and belonging in a meaningful group.

A congregation is a collection of groups. There is, finally, no such thing as a large church. What we call a large church is a collection of small congregations who have enough in common to share the same centralized space and facilities and the same pastor and pastoral staff. The art of serving a large church is, in fact, the art of serving a cooperative parish. With the exception of small congregations that are, in themselves, primary significant relaitonal groups, most local churches are collections of groups.

Indeed, it is possible in long-range planning to diagram the three to five primary relational groups in any congregation. It is important to focus on those groups that provide substantial sharing and caring among the participants and that are dominant groups in the life and mission of the congregation. One might simply diagram them through the use of a connected collection of circles and then provide a brief description of each one. A good deal of the dynamic of that congregation in terms of the sources of stability, change, conflict, and hope can be discovered by a thoughtful study of such a diagram.

It should be observed that new people tend to join new groups. New people in a community tend to search out other people who are comparatively new; new people in a church tend to search out new groups in which they can establish relationships of sharing and caring. The reason for this is very simple. It is easier for new people to establish deeply profound relationships with one another when the network of relationships is still comparatively new, flexible, and in process of development. New groups are those that have been in existence less than five years. Old groups are those that have been in existence more than five years. Whenever a group has been in existence more than five years it has developed a reliable and stable network of relationships. As open and as genuinely caring as that old group seeks to be, it nevertheless takes new people a good deal of time to learn and discover their place in that already fully established network of relationships.

Therefore, it is simply easier and quicker for new people to become part of a sharing and caring group to the extent that it is comparatively new and its network of relationships is not yet fully in place. The corollary to this principle is quite straightforward. Those churches that quit starting new groups are churches that have decided to die. Those churches that thoughtfully and intentionally start a range of new groups are those churches that have decided to grow slowly or rapidly.

It is not the case that the groups cause the growth. Rather, the groups solidify the growth that has already occurred as the result of the outreach in mission and visitation in which the congregation has engaged.

Central to the development of an effective and successful future for a local church, therefore, is its long-range plan to establish significant relational groups. Any new grouping, particularly among young adults, has the possibility of a life of forty years or more. Those groups endure and become the pivotal grouping with which many people live out their full life's pilgrimage. In one church I know of, the Grow class has been in existence for fifty years. It was named the Grow class because, as young couples with very small children, the first members saw themselves engaged in the enormous process of growth. That class now includes a few distinguished persons in their eighties. That class has also been the pivotal primary relational group for most of its members during these past fifty years.

The formula for significant relational groups (Figure 4.1) will help you to decide how many groups it makes sense to begin each year. Not all of the groups that begin will be successful. Indeed, it is probable that one out of three may not succeed.

Some churches fail to start new groups because they have had one or two that have failed. As a matter of fact, it is important to do precisely the opposite. The more groups that have failed, the more important it becomes to intentionally and thoughtfully start an array of new groups. The formula in Figure 4.1 suggests on a conservative basis the number of groups that a church might develop over a period of time.

Caring and Sharing

As a church seeks to start new groups, three developmental principles are important to understand. First, it is important to know that it takes */.* approximately three years for a new group to develop sufficient cohesiveness to endure during its probable life expectancy of forty years. During

Figure 4.1 Significant Relational Groups Formula

1. Number of primary relational groups in church at present   _____
2. The church's total projected increase in participants (constituents and members) per year (see Figure 2.2)   _____
3. Take 80% of projected increase (2) to determine number of people available for new "significant relational groups."
   Note: 20% of new participants will join present ("old") groups for friendship and kinship reasons.   _____
4. Divide number of people available for new groups (3) by 35 to ascertain the potential number of new groups that could be planned each year.   _____
5. Adjust new groups figure (4) so that church is planning new groups on the basis of no more than a 33% ratio to present groups. For example, a church with three present groups might best start only one new group this year. (The exception is a church with only one present group. Fewer conflicts will occur if this church starts *two* new groups this year.)   _____

the first year a new group searches for its identity. During the second year it searches for its leadership and sense of the future. More often than not, during the second year crises develop as that new group begins to put fully in place its leadership and its sense of future direction. Sometimes churches close down a new group during the second year because attendance has fallen off, not as many people are participating, and it looks as though the group is going downhill. As a matter of fact, that may be simply the normal crisis through which any group emerges to have the strength and sense of endurance that comes in the third year.

2. The second principle has to do with key leadership of the new group. Frequently, new groups rotate leadership responsibilities. That may be helpful in the very early stages of the first year. The rotation of leadership responsibilities is really that group's search for the kind of permanent leadership that will be the core of its stability and future direction. Sometime during the second year or early in the third year it will be important for the group to develop some cohesive consensus as to who the key leadership will be for some time to come. Without the stability and reliability of leadership it becomes very difficult for any group to develop the depth of sharing and caring for which most people are

searching. Therefore, the leaders are decisive for the quality of the group that develops.

As a church launches new groups it is important to make available some that build on the natural relational neighborhood in which persons in the community already live, rather than the socioeconomic-cultural neighborhood. It is even less productive to force people into groups based on their geographical neighborhood.

Were a church to think of starting a network of groups across the congregation, the least constructive way to do it would be to organize the membership into geographical zones. The more constructive and creative way to do it would be to invite people to participate in relational groups that build on the natural relationships of friendships and kinships that they have already established within the church.

Wherever persons have not already established those relational ties, the appropriate way to launch a new group is to invite people to one-time or short-term occasions in which they can begin to discover the sense of friendship and kinship that they in fact may be able to develop. A developmental, process approach to starting new groups is more helpful than a unilateral, program approach that presses for group formation too quickly.

People, Not Programs

In this country, the preoccupation of local congregations with programs and activities is deplorable. People win people to Christ; programs do not. People discover people in significant relational groups, not in a merry-go-round of programs and activities.

Some churches become so involved in sponsoring a vast array of programs and activities that they lose sight of the people those programs and activities allegedly serve. Professional staff become preoccupied with advancing their own territory—the programs and activities related to their arena of responsibility—and lose sight of people they started out to serve.

Increasingly, effective and successful congregations have discovered that people are more important than programs—that people reach other people—precisely because all of us search for groups in which we can discover significant relationships of sharing and caring. Effective congregations offer these groups—and start new groups of similar character in thoughtful, helpful ways.

Rating Guide: Significant Relational Groups

Item	Maximum Points	Your Church's Rating
1. Is there an adequate number of groups in relation to the size of the congregation? A church with an average worship attendance of 100 would appropriately have 7 to 10 groups for all ages.	20	_____
2. To what extent do persons discover a strong sense of community in the local church's present groups?	20	_____
3. Is there a sufficient number of new groups in relation to the present and projected size of the membership and constituency? An appropriate ratio would be 1 new group for each 3 present groups.	25	_____
4. To what extent do persons discover a strong sense of community in these new groups?	20	_____
5. Is an adequate number of new groups being planned for the coming several years? (See Figure 4.1.)	15	_____
Total:	100	_____

INSTRUCTIONS:

- Use the information in the chapter as a resource in evaluating your church's rating in each of the listed items.
- Enter the rating numbers in the blanks and then find the total.
- Divide the total of your assessment score by 10 to obtain your church's rating on a scale of 1 to 10.
- Enter that rating on the rating scale for Significant Relational Groups in Figure C.1.

5. Strong Leadership Resources

Leaders and Power

The fifth central characteristic of effective, successful congregations is strong leadership. A local congregation has this key characteristic well enough in place to rank itself 8, 9, or 10 whenever (1) there is a key group of strong leaders, (2) there is a set of strategic objectives these leaders have accomplished and are accomplishing, and (3) there is a good match between the lay leadership and the pastor and staff. Whenever these major components are strongly in place, that congregation has considerable power to advance its future during the coming years of its life and mission.

Strong leadership generates enormous power and momentum to advance a congregation forward. That power is neither dictatorial nor authoritarian, neither oppressive nor domineering. Rather, strong leadership generates power to effectively develop (1) specific concrete missional objectives, (2) pastoral and lay visitation, (3) corporate, dynamic worship, and (4) significant relational groupings. If a church could have only five of the twelve characteristics well in place, it would be these first five that would deliver whichever of the remaining seven that would be important for that church to accomplish its mission in the world.

Leaders and Achievements

Leaders, Not Enablers

In analyzing the extent to which a given local congregation has strong leadership resources, it is useful and helpful to look at eight specific components of this characteristic. The first of these is the extent to which there are leaders, not enablers, in the central positions of leadership in the congregation. The time for leaders has come, the time for enablers has passed. In the churched culture of the 1950s, it was possible for the church to focus on developing enablers. In the unchurched culture of the 1980s it is decisively important that the church focus on developing leaders.

Leaders are those who effectively lead. There may have been a time when it was useful to think of them as enablers; certainly, the management philosophy that centered on the word "enabler" was a major contribution in overcoming the benevolent authoritarian styles of leadership of a number of pastors and key laypersons. To that extent, the enabler movement has been useful.

However, that movement has seen its day. Whenever the concept of enabler has been linked with nondirective counseling techniques, the local church has suffered from dysfunctional leadership. The reactive, responsive, process-centered style of leadership present in many local congregations contributes significantly to those congregations being declining or dying congregations.

It is appropriate to focus both on process and on responsive considerations in any style of leadership. At the same time, it is decisive that leaders lead the congregation forward toward the thoughtful accomplishment and achievement of substantive objectives. That means that leaders are active as well as responsive. That means that leaders share their own sense of direction and vision as well as simply enabling others to share theirs.

In no sense am I advocating that leaders should become dictatorial and authoritarian, even in the most benevolent ways. But I am strongly against those who see themselves as enablers whenever they use their enabler philosophy as a cop-out to avoid sharing their own agenda, direction, and vision straightforwardly, or to manipulate the decision-making process in covert ways. In short, local congregations need more leaders and fewer enablers. The extent to which there are potential thoughtful and responsible leaders present in a congregation is the extent to which that congregation is on its way to being able to rank itself as 8, 9, or 10 on this characteristic.

A Balance of Life Strengths

In assessing whether or not a given congregation has strong leadership resources, it is important to analyze the extent to which those who have strong leadership strengths have available to them people with complementary strengths: supportive, analytical, discerning, and relational. A healthy congregation will have strong leadership resources representing a balance of life strengths.

Consider, for example, a football team: it needs the leadership of a good quarterback but would be ineffective if *all* the players were quarterbacks. Players with complementary skills as guards, ends, and tackles provide the balance needed to function effectively. Imagine a team with three first-string quarterbacks and with guards, ends, and tackles who are third-string. That team is not likely to be effective in its mission to win games.

The Quality of the Objectives

Any analysis of the extent to which a local congregation has strong leadership resources must focus on the quality of the objectives toward which the leaders are working. The quality of these objectives is generally fairly high whenever the following criteria have been met.

1. The objectives are written.
2. The leaders have a strong sense of ownership of the objectives.
3. The objectives are specific and measurable.
4. The objectives have realistic time horizons.
5. The objectives are concrete and achievable.
6. The objectives mutually reinforce one another in a complementary fashion.

In addition to these six criteria about the quality of a local congregation's objectives, it is important to note that the fewer objectives a congregation has, the more likely it is to be moving forward with strong leadership. The art of having high-quality objectives is the art of focusing on the two out of ten strategic objectives that will deliver 80 percent of the results. Generally, a congregation that has too many objectives is a congregation that nurtures a mediocre range of leadership resources. The multiplicity of the objectives engenders a sense of failure, low self-esteem, and lack of confidence.

Accomplishments, Not Activities

The more activities a congregation has, the less likely it is to have strong leadership resources. The more a congregation has achieved, the more likely it is to have strong leadership resources. It is difficult to suggest which comes first—the set of accomplishments, or the strong leadership. But it is clearly the case that the greater the number of activities, the greater the likelihood that a congregation is in the process of weakening its leadership resources.

There is, of course, some relationship between accomplishments and activities. This appropriate and limited relationship has to do with whether the activities move toward accomplishments. Too many churches plan, sponsor, and promote activities that have no direct correlation with any of the objectives and accomplishments toward which they are strategically headed. Activities should never be seen as ends in themselves. Activities are those critical events that advance toward the accomplishment of strategic objectives.

The Combination of Competency and Continuity

Whenever a local church has successfully combined competency of leadership skills with continuity of those leadership skills, it has substantive leadership resources. The primary focus should not be on commitment. The focus should be primarily on competency, then compassion, and then—and only then—commitment. Too many churches focus on who's committed as they think about who they want to ask to serve in major leadership positions. It is more important to focus on who will be competent, who is also compassionate, and who also has some degree of commitment.

Further, many churches rotate their leadership too frequently to achieve strong continuity of competent leaders. There is a myth that leaders want to rotate off from leadership positions at the end of three years. In many churches it takes nearly three years to develop a given leadership post. By the time the person has achieved a functioning competency in the post, that person has rotated off and the congregation is forced to start over again.

Some pastors and some lay leaders promoted the idea of rotation under the guise of giving everyone a chance to be a leader and of wanting people to have a year off so they would not get burned out. Actually, some of these pastors and lay leaders were using the rotational principle to avoid the development of "power blocs" of leaders in a congregation. Frankly, the lack of continuity of competent leadership is a more dangerous and difficult situation for a local church than the possibility it might have to deal with a power bloc.

No responsible institution rotates its major leadership every three years; most effective and successful institutions develop long-term continuity for their most competent leaders. Further, by definition, a competent leader is one who leads in a participatory way, not one who leads in an authoritarian and dictatorial fashion. The best thing to do with those who tend toward dictatorial and authoritarian leadership styles is never to put them in any position of leadership. But the fear that some of those people might emerge as a power bloc is no excuse for rotating out of principal leadership positions those very competent leaders who have strong objective-setting and process-development skills.

The Ratio of 1 to 15

In analyzing whether a given congregation has strong leadership resources well in place, the sixth factor to assess is that of the ratio of competent leaders to the number of people in the congregation. A rule of thumb would be one competent leader to fifteen members and constituents who are active participants in the life and mission of the congregation. I did not say one leader in relation to fifteen members; that would be a foolish notion. It would be foolish because there are a host of members who live out of town, whose address is unknown, or who are "dyed-in-the-wool" inactive in that congregation. It is appropriate to study the ratio of leaders to the number of people who are reasonably active members and constituents in the congregation.

It is important to observe that this 1 to 15 ratio is only a rule of thumb and should not be taken literally or absolutely. Moreover, the focus should be on whether or not we have one out of fifteen reasonably active members and constituents who have the *potential* of being strong leaders in the life and mission of this congregation. Right now, they may not be actually engaged in leadership responsibilities in the congregation. It is more important to see what potential there is in terms of this ratio than it is to measure what the ratio is at present.

Strong Pastoral and Staff Leadership

The seventh factor to consider is the extent to which the local congregation has strong pastoral and staff leadership. In most congregations that means looking at whether or not the pastor brings strong leadership skills to that post. Such leadership skills enable the pastor to focus on major planning, policy, personnel, program, and financial objectives and decisions that shape the future of that local congregation's mission and outreach.

The pastor does not have strong leadership skills if the pastor's decisions deal with detailed matters like whether there will be yellow or blue name tags at next Wednesday night's covered-dish dinner. The pastor and staff who compulsively focus on details lack strong leadership skills. It is the pastor who concentrates on major objectives and major decisions having to do with the congregation's strategic priorities that will make it possible for that congregation to develop strong leadership resources.

Recognition and Reward

The eighth factor to consider in an assessment of whether or not a local congregation has strong leadership resources is the system of recognition and rewards. The more the emphasis of that recognition and reward system is on positive reinforcement, the more likely the congregation will be to have strong leadership resources. The more that recognition and reward system is preoccupied with negative reinforcement, the more likely that congregation is to have weak, mediocre leaders who suffer from low self-esteem and lack of confidence.

The more the recognition and reward system tells people what they are not doing, the more likely it is to establish a sense of latent hostility and guilt in the congregation. This sense of hostility and guilt immobilizes people and prevents them from developing their creative, constructive competencies to deliver genuine leadership. Congregations that have put into place a positive recognition and reward system nurture leaders who have wisdom, judgment, vision, creativity, and compassion as they provide effective leadership.

Directions for Development

Lay Leadership

Mission and leaders.   Four directions are useful in the development of lay leadership strength within a congregation. The first of these is to develop a solid balance between mission and leaders. A good objective for many local congregations would be to deploy approximately 50 percent of its leaders in mission and outreach in the community and the other 50 percent in the accomplishment of programs within the local church itself. Some congregations have the noble objective that they will give 50 percent of their income to missions and spend 50 percent on themselves. That is an interesting and occasionally useful objective, but it is amazing to me that comparatively few congregations apply the same principle to the way in which they deploy their leaders. Indeed, very little thought is given by most congregations to the deployment of their leaders, let alone to deploying some of their leaders in mission and some within the congregation itself.

Increasingly, the unchurched culture in which we live will invite local congregations to make intentional decisions about the number and strength with which they deploy their leadership. For example, a given congregation may have a total of thirty effective leaders. It would be regrettable if twenty-five of those leaders were preoccupied with programs and activities within the local church and only five asked to serve in mission and outreach in the community. In our unchurched culture, it would be far more appropriate for ten to fifteen of them to have been invited to deliver their leadership skills in mission and outreach in the community and the remainder to carry forward the programs and activities of the local church.

Too many local churches have an "inside-the-church-walls" approach to leadership deployment, and it is precisely because of this "inside" deployment of leadership that many congregations are declining or dying. They have used the skills of their key leaders on maintenance activities, financial activities, and membership activities and have not had the vision to invite a substantial number of their key leaders to focus on mission in the community.

Leaders and Program. A second key direction for the development of strong leadership resources is to discover the number of leaders a local congregation has and then to build the mission and program of that church in direct relation to the number and strengths of its leaders. Unfortunately, most churches decide what they plan to do in the way of programs and activities as though they had an unlimited reservoir of leaders. Further, they make the foolish assumption that they would have an unlimited reservoir if "only the people in this congregation were more committed." The fallacy in that assumption is that there is no necessary correlation between competency and commitment; it is foolish to assume that simply because people are committed they are therefore competent. They may be simply committed.

Whenever a local congregation builds its program and activities without taking seriously how many leaders are present and with what range of competencies, that local church sets itself up for failure. Some churches are sufficiently masochistic that they enjoy the sense of failure and low self-esteem that such a process engenders. But a healthy congregation that wants to develop strong leadership resources first analyzes the number of key leaders and the competencies those key leaders have. It then develops the mission and program that best match the number and competency of the leaders in the congregation.

It is the old football analogy. You *first* discover the number of competent players who have shown up for practice and *then* you design the plays to match. No wise football coach does it the other way around. No wise church does it the other way around, either.

Effective, successful churches assess their leadership strengths and develop their mission and program commensurately. Those churches that do not do this tend to commit themselves to a "filling of the empty slots" and to a disastrous disarray of disappointment and failure in their mission and program.

Competencies and Authority. The third direction for the development of strong leadership resources is to match the competencies of the key leaders with solid responsibility and authority. If a local congregation wants its competent leaders to function effectively, it is important that that congregation and pastor deliver to these leaders both responsibilities *and* the authority appropriate to the responsibilities. Too many pastors and too many congregations ask competent leaders to assume certain responsibilities without giving them the necessary authority to fulfill their responsibilities. Never give people responsibilities unless you are also willing to give them the necessary authority.

Much of the frustration between competent lay leaders and pastors comes at precisely this point; many pastors are unwilling to share authority with their key leaders. They want them to have the responsibilities, but they want to reserve the authority for themselves as pastors. Pastors may do this partly because they are uncertain or insecure in their own sense of authority; hence, they do a good deal of "turf protecting." Some pastors even develop almost a caste system delineating prerogatives of the pastor and the laity in the congregation. Indeed, it is often especially these pastors who talk a pretty good game of "theology of the laity," when in fact, they are unwilling to share authority with their laity. The direct result is the weakening of leadership resources and a decreased sense of accomplishment in mission and program.

Characteristics of the Individual. The fourth direction that will facilitate the development of strong leadership resources is to look for those key characteristics in people that indicate their competence and capacity to be solid leaders. The following characteristics are important factors to consider as one matches a given person with a given leadership responsibility in the life and mission of a congregation:

- Specific competencies and skills that match well with the job specifications and objectives that you hope will be accomplished in the particular leadership position
- General competencies in work patterns
- Compassion in human relationships
- Commitment to the specific leadership post
- Commitment to this congregation
- Committment to the church's mission in the world
- Life strengths in productive situations
- Life strengths in stress and conflict situations
- The person's role in prior groups of significant relationships
- The individual's personal character and self-esteem

Although one might develop an even longer list of critical factors to look for in matching leaders with leadership positions, these factors are a useful range to consider. At this juncture, the basic point is to consider whether or not a given person has at least eight of these factors well in place and therefore would be a good match with the given leadership position. Too often the local congregation places people where the local church needs them to fill some slot, or where they think the person has an interest, whether or not that person really has competencies needed to do the job.

The Pastor and the Staff

Six key points are worth mentioning as the local congregation seeks to build strong pastoral and staff leadership. The first of these is about developing a staff.

1. *Staff Development.* As need for additional staff members is felt, it is important that a team of competent professionals be built with an ordered and reasoned plan. An appropriate order to bring staff on board would be as follows:

First, a pastor who becomes a shepherd, a leader, and a preacher with the congregation.

Next, a director of music, whether part-time or full-time, who develops the music components of the congregation's corporate, dynamic services of worship. Generally speaking, this person would come on board as the second key staff person, regardless of the size of the church. If only one thing can go well in a given local church, it is important that worship go extraordinarily well.

Next, a church secretary or a church administrator. This person can nearly double the effectiveness of the pastor. This is particularly so whenever this person brings executive secretarial and administrative competencies to the post.

Next, a director of program. This person delivers the development and coordination of the total program of the church. This person may specialize in given age ranges or particular group functions. At the same time, this staff person shares an overall, comprehensive perspective of the development of the total program.

Last, a director of mission and outreach. The titles may vary from one church to another. It is important, nevertheless, for there to be a key staff person, depending on the size of the church, who devotes substantive portions of his or her time to the mission and outreach of the congregation in the community.

From one church to the next, the development of given staff positions may take a slightly different order. However, the order mentioned above is a useful sequence for a majority of congregations who are seeking to grow or are already rapidly growing. Certainly, given congregations have unique circumstances and must appropriately develop the sequence of their own staff positions in ways that advance the objectives in mission and program toward which they are headed.

2. *Total Persons Served.* It is important to build the staff in relation to the total persons served, not simply the membership alone. Many congregations think in terms of the number of staff they ought to have in relation to the number of members they have. Basically, as was seen earlier, local congregations consist of three major groups: (1) members, (2) constituents, and (3) persons served in mission. The best way to develop a staff is to put in place the number of staff who can best serve the total number of people (members, constituents, and persons served in mission) with which a church works and shares in the course of a given year. One reason many staffs are overworked, battle-fatigued, and burned out is that congregations have brought on board staff based on the number of members without any sense that the congregation is dealing with far more people in a year's time than simply its members.

3. *The 2 to 1 Ratio.* The most effective and least expensive ratio is that of two support staff for each pastoral or program staff person. That does not mean to suggest that these two support staff necessarily report directly to a specific pastoral or program staff person. Rather, it is to suggest that wherever a local church has a ratio of one support staff to two pastoral staff they in fact have three secretaries instead of one. This typical pattern in many congregations—one pastor, one associate pastor, and one church secretary—means that the pastor and the associate pastor are doing more paperwork than they have any right to do, and that paperwork prevents them from doing the peoplework that it is important for them to do.

The most effective and least expensive staff ratio would be to have one pastor, one executive secretary, and one clerk typist. In terms of budget, that will be less expensive. In terms of effectiveness, that will be extraordinarily more effective. A competent executive secretary will nearly double the effectiveness of the pastor, and the clerk typist will deliver the routine secretarial duties that free the executive secretary to do both people work and paperwork of an administrative nature. In turn, that will free the pastor to focus on shepherding, leadership, and preaching—the three key responsibilities important for a pastor to fulfill.

Another advantage to this ratio can be seen by looking at the four kinds of associate pastors that are commonly seen:

1. Apprentice associates: These people are generally with a given congregation for two to three years. At the present time it will cost most local congregations a total of $40,000 to $50,000 to have an associate pastor over two years. Then, that associate pastor, having been trained by a local church, will generally move on. It is too expensive and not effective enough to consider having an apprentice pastor in very many local churches.

2. Professional associate pastors: These are hard to find and hard to come by. Wherever a local church has been able to secure one, that local church has been richly blessed. In our culture it is easier to find a professional executive secretary than it is to find a professional associate pastor.

3. Retired pastors: Many local congregations have found it possible to deliver pastoral back-up to the pastor as the church grows larger by asking a retired pastor to serve on staff. Two rules of thumb are important. First, bring onto the staff only those retired pastors who have been good shepherds in their active ministry. The fact that a pastor is retired does not mean he is a competent good shepherd. It may just mean he's retired. The second rule is to bring the pastor on board for a one-year or two-year contract, renewable at the mutual discretion of the church and the retired associate. Do not bring a retired person on board "until death us do part."

4. Incompetent associates: Generally speaking, this is the largest group of associate pastors available to a local church. This does not mean to suggest that all associate pastors are incompetent. Certainly, some associate pastors are apprentices, some are professionals, and some are retired associates. But, regrettably, a substantial range of persons who have found their way into associate pastor

positions do not have substantive competencies for ministry. If only such associate pastors are available to serve a given church, that church would be better off employing a competent executive secretary or church administrator.

Overall, a church would do well, as it develops its staff, to put in place a strong support staff as it adds various pastoral and program staff.

4. *Life Expectancy.* When a local congregation brings on board a pastor or any member of a staff, it is valuable for that congregation to bring on board only those who have a probability of serving seven or more years in the post. To put that another way, whenever a staff position experiences one turnover in a seven-year period, it becomes cost-*in*effective for that church. As an example, let's assume that the position of church secretary has a turnover once in a seven-year period. That means that the local church had a year of entry and a year of exit with the first church secretary. It will have a year of entry and a year of exit with the second church secretary. If that church pays an average annual salary of $12,000 for the position, that means that it has just cost the church four years of entry and exit, totaling $48,000, to achieve three years ($36,000) of productive work. It would be far better for a congregation to pay solid salaries that contribute to continuity in a position than nickel-and-dime salaries that contribute to high turnover, particularly in support staff positions.

It costs less money over a seven-year period to pay competitive, substantial salaries that avoid a high turnover rate than it does to nickel-and-dime the salaries of pastoral and staff positions year by year in a local church. Pastor-parish committees would do well to study this. Frequently, the most productive years of a pastor begin in year five, six, or seven. Likewise, the most productive years of any staff person begin about year five, six, or seven. It is cost-effective to pay higher salaries year by year over the long haul. It is most wasteful to pay low salaries year by year and have a high turnover rate.

5. *The 40 to 60 Ratio.* In many medium-sized and large congregations, the appropriate ratio of budget for pastor and staff is 40 to 60 percent. That is, approximately 40 to 60 percent of the total operating budget is best invested in the salaries and benefits of the pastor and the staff. As a matter of fact, in small congregations the percentage is closer to 70 to 80 percent. As a church grows from a small congregation to a medium-sized congregation, the percentage of total budget that goes to pastoral and staff salaries tends to drop. As a church moves from a medium-sized to a large congregation, that percentage tends to drop even more.

When in my role as a church consultant I have found salaries totaling

60 percent of the operating budget, one of two things has generally been true. First, the local congregation has positioned itself with a very competent staff in order to become rapidly growing or stable and growing. The second possibility is that it is an inner city congregation whose days of growth have passed for one reason or another but which continues to have a number of staff positions in place in relation to the size they once were rather than the size they now are.

Whenever I have found the salary ratio to be 40 percent, one of two things has generally been true. First, the church has minimal staff in relation to its mission and program, which thereby creates an overworked, battle-fatigued, burned-out staff and a church that has positioned itself to be declining. Or second, I have found churches that have major stewardship programs with a range of giving so strong that the percentage of budget toward salaries is appropriately set around 40 percent.

6. *Merit Increases*.   The sixth factor that contributes to the development of a competent pastor and staff has to do with the kinds of recognition and rewards delivered to them. In terms of financial recognition and rewards, it is important for the local congregation to distinguish between cost-of-living salary adjustments, merit increases, and major merit increases. If the inflation factor in a given year is 8 percent and the congregation decides to give to its staff an 8 percent raise, that congregation has decided not to give its pastor and staff *any* raise. The cost-of-living salary adjustment simply enables the pastor and the staff to have the same purchasing power this coming year that they have had in the current year.

For example, in a given church a pastor was receiving a salary of $20,000. The church decided that it was appropriate that the pastor receive an 8 percent raise because the inflation factor in that area of the country had been 8 percent during the present year. Therefore, the church gave the pastor what they described as an 8 percent raise. That meant that the pastor's salary would be $21,600. But, in actual purchasing power, the $21,600 could buy no more goods and services in the coming year than the $20,000 the pastor had been receiving in the current year. Cost-of-living salary adjustments are best described not as raises but as adjustments for the rise in the cost of living.

In addition to these cost-of-living adjustments, it is important that the congregation share with its pastor and staff appropriate merit increases, including major merit increases. Those staff persons who have solidly accomplished the objectives that they sought to achieve should receive merit increases that give recognition and honor to the work they have accomplished. Those staff persons who have accomplished their objectives in extraordinarily creative and courageous ways should be given major merit increases. All of this is to suggest that there is a clear correlation between the productivity of the pastor and the staff and the extent to which the congregation recognizes that productivity in terms of cost-of-living salary adjustments, merit increases, and major merit increases.

Leaders and the Future

As leaders share substantive leadership strengths on behalf of the congregation's mission and program, the future becomes the present reality and the present reality of accomplishments and achievements advances us toward the future God has both prepared and promised for that congregation. It is not simply the case that "our young people are the leaders of our church for tomorrow." It is the case that the *present* has the power to shape what tomorrow looks like. To be sure, there are certain limitations to that future that must be taken seriously. At the same time, the congregation that has discovered, developed, and deployed its leadership resources has before it a future of mission, hope, and accomplishment. This will mean much in the lives of people as they seek to live out this earthly pilgrimage with responsibility and integrity.

Rating Guide: Strong Leadership Resources

Item	Maximum Points	Your Church's Rating
1. To what extent are leaders in your church leaders, not enablers?	15	_____
2. Is there an appropriate balance of life strengths among the leaders?	10	_____
3. Is there a complementary quality to the objectives?	15	_____
4. To what extent is the focus on accomplishments, not activities?	10	_____
5. Is there a strong combination of competency and continuity?	10	_____
6. Is the ratio of 1 to 15 met?	10	_____
7. Is there strong pastoral and staff leadership?	15	_____
8. Are proper recognition and rewards given?	15	_____
Total:	100	_____

INSTRUCTIONS:

- Use the information in the chapter as a resource in evaluating your church's rating in each of the listed items.
- Enter the rating numbers in the blanks and then find the total.
- Divide the total of your assessment score by 10 to obtain your church's rating on a scale of 1 to 10.
- Enter that rating on the rating scale for Strong Leadership Resources in Figure C.1.

6. Streamlined Structure and Solid, Participatory Decision Making

Decisions and Structure

The sixth central characteristic of effective, successful churches has to do with decisions and structure. Those congregations that have a solid, participatory decision-making process and a streamlined organizational structure can be ranked 8, 9, or 10 on this characteristic. That is, solid decisions are made, ownership and openness to all opinions are high, the process is as important as the decisions, and the organizational structure is streamlined and constructive.

It is important to observe that there is a direct correlation between decision making and structure. A solid, participatory decision-making process contributes to a streamlined organizational structure and a streamlined organizational structure facilitates solid, participatory decision making. Congregations that have a cumbersome decision-making process will be likely to have a complex organizational structure. By the same token, their complex organizational structure will contribute directly to the cumbersomeness of the decision-making process.

Decisions, Not Discussion

Solid Decisions

The decision-making process is solid when the decisions demonstrate wisdom, a sense of priorities, and character. First, the most effective decision-making process is one that contributes to the development of wise decisions and thoughtful directions for the life and mission of a congregation. Sometimes a congregation develops decisions that are simply faddish—that is, they reflect some popular fad among churches across the country. Sometimes churches develop decisions that are immature—that is, decisions that are hastily reached on the spur of the moment and reflect an adolescent rather than an adult sense of judgment and discernment. Sometimes churches develop decisions that are simply stupid—that is, the decisions reflect neither wisdom nor common sense. Frequently, such decisions are made because someone has sold that church "a bill of goods." Generally, the decision-making process can be said to be solid when most of the decisions reached reflect sound wisdom and thoughtful common sense.

Second, the decision-making process can be said to be solid whenever the decisions focus on the important priorities rather than the urgent trivialities. There are four groups of decisions that must be considered by a local congregation. Matters that are both important and urgent are #1 decisions. Matters that are important but not urgent are #2 decisions. Urgent but not important matters are #3 decisions. Matters that are neither important nor urgent are #4 decisions. Many congregations live out their lives together focusing on #3 and #4 decisions rather than the #1 and #2 decisions they should be concerned with. Then they wonder why they are declining or dying congregations. Effective congregations invest most of their decision-making time on those matters that qualify as #1 and #2 decisions.

Third, a local congregation should focus on decisions that are needed as well as those that are wanted. The best way to describe this is to say that the decision-making process is solid whenever there is character to the decisions. That is, the decisions reflect courage and backbone rather than simply a willy-nilly effort to please everyone—which usually ends up pleasing no one. The maturity of the decision-making process in a congregation is directly related to the capacity of that congregation to make those decisions that they *need* to make as well as those decisions that they want to make.

Participatory

The effective congregation has a participatory decision-making process whenever three things are well in place: ownership, openness, and a dynamic relationship between the informal and formal arenas of participation. The decision-making process is participatory whenever there is a high degree of ownership both for the process and for the decisions reached. This is not to suggest that everyone agrees with the process or with the decisions that result from the process. Rather, it is to suggest that overall there is a sense of genuine and authentic ownership for the way that local congregation goes about making decisions and for the results of the decisions that the process yields. Indeed, the process should nurture and facilitate ownership, and the decisions that result reinforce the high degree of ownership that the process has nurtured.

The process is participatory whenever it is open and inclusive rather than closed and restricted. That does not mean to suggest that every person in a congregation should be forced to participate in every decision that needs to be made in that congregation. There existed some years ago a fad for total consensus for every decision. Pastors and key leaders of congregations should disabuse themselves of the notion that everyone in the congregation should be included in every decision—or that everyone in that local congregation even *wants* to be included in every decision. In fact, most people do not. Rather, they want the sense of openness and inclusiveness that makes it easy for them to share their own judgment and wisdom on a given matter if they want to do so.

Certainly, everyone in a congregation should be encouraged to participate in the central strategic decisions that affect the destiny of the congregation. Beyond that, it is important that a streamlined organizational structure facilitate given committees and groups making decisions assigned to them and to their responsibility and authority. What most people do not like is the sense that the decision-making process is closed and restrictive; what they further do not like is to be pressed into participating in minor decisions in which they have no interest. It is important that the key leaders and the pastor develop an open and inclusive process. People will then understand that is it a participatory decision-making process and will be able to participate when they want to.

Decision-making is participatory whenever there is a constructive interrelationship between the informal network of particpation and the formal organizational structure for decision making. In some local congregations, the pastor and/or a group of key leaders may so formalize decision making that there is no connection whatsoever between the formal committee meetings in which the decisions are ratified and the informal network of participation in the church and community grapevine where the decisions are discussed and reflected on before they are brought to a formal arena for ratification.

Pastors would do well to understand that most decisions are arrived at in informal conversations and settings and then simply ratified in the more formal arena of the committee meeting itself. That should not be viewed as subterfuge or as an unusual pattern of behavior. Indeed, most people make most of the decisions they make in everyday life in informal settings and informal discussions. When it comes to making decisions in the life and mission of the congregation, they are simply following the same behavior patterns. From my point of view, it is important that people have sufficient lead time to informally discuss with one another the decisions of major importance that they are being called upon to make in the formal gathering of a major committee in the church.

Decision-Making Process

Three factors about the decision-making process are important to analyze and evaluate. First, it is important to assess the extent to which the decision-making process facilitates decisions, not discussion. The purpose of the process is not extensive discussion; the purpose of an effective process is the development of wise decisions. The process should encourage sufficient discussion to make possible such wise decisions, but not an overabundance of discussion. Indeed, some in leadership positions become so captured by the notion of process that they nurture discussion to the point of overkill, which finally yields frustrated and hurried decisions in which a congregation or committee has little confidence. It is important that the process move the discussion forward at a reasonable pace, so that wise decisions are made.

Second, the decision-making process is effective whenever the leaders have as much conern for the importance of the process as they do for the resulting decisions. The methodology by which a congregation achieves decisions is as important as the decisions themselves. An adequate and appropriate balance between the process and the decisions should be the strong concern of the key leaders and the pastor. To be sure, finally the decision-making process drives toward decisions, not discussion. It drives toward accomplishments and achievements, not simply activities. But it does so with a thoughtful understanding that the process being built will facilitate future decisions and directions for the church.

Third, the decision-making process is effective in direct relation to the way in which the congregation responds to conflict. The local church that never experiences conflict is not likely to have an effective decision-making process. Generally, churches that do not experience conflict have either a pastor or key leaders who have developed an artful domination of the decisions made. They may have developed this sense of domination through overt force or covert methods of manipulation.

The dynamics of stability, change, conflict, and hope are persistent, useful, creative dynamics in the life of the congregation. It is important that the local congregation develop the capacity to resolve rather than repress conflict. Congregations have an effective decision-making process to the extent that the members of the congregation—in the midst of conflict over a given matter—can respond to one another with mutual trust, respect, and integrity. A discussion of the principles and purposes rather than an attack on personalities demonstrates an effective methodology for dealing with conflict.

This is not to say that people will not shout at each other. Sometimes they will. This is not to say that people will not sometimes spread gossip about their opponents in the conflict. They frequently will do so. But it *is* to say that over the long haul, a congregation that has an effective decision-making process is one in which members share with each other an inviting sense of mutual trust, mutual respect, and integrity for one another's position, even amidst a raging conflict.

Streamlined Organizational Structure

Three principles contribute to the organizational structure being streamlined. The first of these flows from a foundational principle about the number of committees and the number of people that it is useful to have on each. It is important that a congregation have enough committees to develop wise decisions and strong achievements and that each committee have enough members to allow their complementary life strengths to yield creative decisions and effective action.

The purpose of the organizational structure in the local church is not to "involve" people. Years ago, the myth was spawned that the way to involve people is to put them on a committee, and the results of that myth have been among the most harmful and destructive factors contributing to many congregations' status as declining or dying churches.

The purpose of the church is to involve people in God's mission in the world, to involve them in worship that is corporate and dynamic and in a group wherein they experience significant relationships of sharing and caring. The central driving purpose of the church is not to involve people in committee meeting after committee meeting. Indeed, it is highly possible for a member of a congregation to be significantly involved in the church's mission in the world, significantly involved in worship, and significantly involved in a major group of solid relationships and to invest very little time serving on committees.

It is regrettable that local congregations consume so much of an individual's time in committee meetings that they have very little time left over to participate in that church's mission in the world. Effective congregations conserve their members' time by developing the most minimal and streamlined organizational structure possible, so that people can be involved substantively and responsibly in the total life and mission of the church.

The second principle is what I call the 20-30-50 rule. Twenty percent of the decisions made in the local church are strategic decisions that will accomplish 80 percent of the results. This 20 percent should be made by a very wide representation of persons in the congregation.

Thirty percent of the decisions made should be appropriately delegated to key leaders and chairpersons of given committees. Fifty percent of the decisions made should be delegated to smaller task forces and specific individuals who have been delegated both responsibility for and authority over those matters. In short, the 20-30-50 rule nurtures a strong process of delegation wherein appropriate decisions are made by those who have been given the responsibility and authority to make them.

The third principle contributing to a streamlined organizational structure is the interrelationship of committees and community. Most people participate in the life and mission of a congregation in order to discover a sense of community. That is, they bring with them to a congregation their deep life's search for roots, place, and belonging. They come looking for community, and we instead put them on a committee. To some extent, people will put up with being on committees insofar as they have discovered community. It is worth observing that the liveliest times in committee meetings are generally before and after the meetings when people stand around visiting with one another—sharing with one another a sense of community, a sense of friendship, and a sense of fellowship. It is important that members of committees develop some sense of community with one another. It is even more important that the individuals on a given committee discover a significant relational group in which they are participating on a long-term, year-after-year basis.

It is not the final purpose of the committee to deliver community. It is the purpose of the committee to develop wise decisions and accomplish major goals. At the same time, the creative committee is one that assesses the extent to which each person on the committee has discovered community at some point in the life of the congregation. Further, it is important that the leaders of the committee develop at least minimal relationships of community. That will frankly facilitate the committee staying together in the tough times of hard decisions amidst major conflicts. There should be at least a minimal interaction between the dynamics of committee and community in any given group in the local church.

Effective Decisions

Anxiety Level

Local congregations tend to make more effective decisions when they take seriously the anxiety level present within the congregation. Most of the time a person's anxiety level has a natural ebb and flow. Surprise a person with a new proposal, and that individual's anxiety level skyrockets. The result is that the individual becomes preoccupied with getting his anxiety level back down to normal. What caused the anxiety level to skyrocket was the new proposal; thus, the individual may reject the new proposal, not because he or she is inherently against it, but in order to get the anxiety level back down to normal.

Major proposals should not be surprises. It is important that major proposals be shared tentatively and thoughtfully, giving people sufficient time to mull them over. Frequently, very good proposals are rejected because they have been hurriedly and hastily shared with people who have then been asked for an immediate decision. Major proposals may need several weeks or months of "mulling over" before people can bring their anxiety level down to normal and deal with the proposal itself.

Committee Meetings

Most effective committee meetings begin on time, have a stated agenda shared in advance, and end on time. Too many committee meetings have a beginning time but no ending time. It should be clear to all concerned that the committee meeting will end at a specific time.

The most effective committee meetings last from thirty minutes to an hour. Occasionally, it makes sense for a committee meeting to last as long as an hour and a half. Generally speaking, evening committee meetings that last longer than an hour and a half are on their way downhill very quickly. Many committees get into their major hassles and arguments because they have met for too long, everyone is tired, and people are interested in going home, and yet the end of the committee meeting does not seem to be in sight. It is precisely in those settings that the nagging, the pettiness, the bickering, and the personal abuse emerge. It is important, therefore, to begin on time and to end on time and to clearly announce the beginning and ending times.

Moreover, it is important that people have the chance to know in advance what decisions they will be called upon to make. This will enable them to deal with their anxiety levels; further, it will enable them to creatively and constructively think through the best alternatives related to a given decision. Most people will invest time in thinking through to their best judgment on a given decision if they know in advance the nature of the decision they will be asked to make.

Follow-Through

When a committee has met and has achieved wise, thoughtful decisions it has accomplished two things: (1) it has met and (2) it has made wise, thoughtful decisions. That is all the committee has done. Clearly, those two things are important. But one cannot assume that because the committee has met and made wise, thoughtful decisions that it has therefore accomplished anything. It's a little like a pastor who assumes that because he has preached a sermon on a given topic he has done something about the matter. No, all that has happened is that a sermon has been preached. The work that will put in place the achievements and accomplishments in relation to the decisions is yet to be done.

It is important, therefore, that committees have effective follow-through mechanisms that nurture the individual members of the committees through to the accomplishment of their respective tasks. Two suggestions will be useful here. First, it will be helpful for the secretary of the committee to put in the mail the next day a one-page list of the decisions that were made in the committee meeting and who will do what, by when, in relation to each decision. It is not important that the secretary develop narrative minutes of everything that is said. To achieve results, it is far more important that the secretary share a one-page set of minutes describing the decisions made and the specific responsibilities of individuals.

A second suggestion will also be helpful. It is important to give people responsibility, authority, and accountability for the tasks they have volunteered to accomplish. Frequently, committees give responsibilities to an individual but not the appropriate authority to deal with those responsibilities. Even more frequently, a committee may give an individual both responsibility and accountability but no authority.

It is important to observe that authority and accountability are given to an individual rather than "laid on that individual." Responsible persons want to know to whom they are accountable for the responsibilities and authority they have. Straight-line accountability is more useful than multiple lines of accountability. Thus, it is important that the committee help the individual member know to whom he or she is accountable for the responsibilities and authority that individual has.

Decisions and Directions

Insofar as a congregation has a steamlined structure and solid, participatory decision making, that congregation is likely to move forward with confidence and competence in the direction that will best put in place its solid destiny as a missional church. The power of wise decisions in a participatory process gives genuine momentum to the capabilities and compentencies present within the members and constituents of that congregation. A streamlined organizational structure facilitates the straightforward development, deployment, and delegation of responsibilities, authority, and accountability so that effective accomplishments and achievements can occur. This relational characteristic is decisive in facilitating the development of effective mission and responsible success in a local church.

Rating Guide: Solid, Participatory Decision Making

Item	Maximum Points	Your Church's Rating
1. To what extent are wise, thoughtful decisions developed in relation to important priorities?	25	_____
2. Is there a strong sense of ownership and openness in terms of the decision-making process?	25	_____
3. Does the decision-making process facilitate helping the local church resolve conflict?	25	_____
4. Is the organizational structure streamlined in relation to the local church's strategic priorities?	25	_____
Total:	100	_____

INSTRUCTIONS:

- Use the information in the chapter as a resource in evaluating your church's rating in each of the listed items.

- Enter the rating numbers in the blanks and then find the total.

- Divide the total of your assessment score by 10 to obtain your church's rating on a scale of 1 to 10.

- Enter that rating on the rating scale for Solid, Participatory Decision Making in Figure C.1.

7. Several Competent Programs and Activities

Programs and People

People win people. Programs do not reach people; people reach people. There is a myth among some churches that the more programs and activities a church can offer, the more people it will reach in the community. The likelihood of that happening is extraordinarily remote.

The more programs and activities the church offers, the more fatigued and overworked the leaders and pastor of that congregation become. It is simply not the case that effective, successful congregations necessarily offer a full range of programs and activities for all ages and all sorts and conditions of people. Many churches assume that the more programs they offer, the more purpose statements they write, the more pieces of paper they send to households through the postal service, the more effective and successful they will become. That simply is not the case.

To be sure, effective and successful congregations tend to have two or three programs that are respected in the community as being solidly competent and outstanding as "services" to a wide range of people in that community. A congregation could rank this central characteristic as an 8, 9, or 10 if it has one or two, or perhaps as many as three, such competent programs as a part of its life and mission.

Programs and the Community

Standards and Criteria

The competence of a congregation's major programs is measured by the communitywide standards of competence for that kind of program. Regrettably, too many congregations have a "soft" analytical and evaluative perspective as they assess their major programs. They frequently evaluate their programs through rose-colored glasses, based on their own uncritical self-satisfaction with what they have developed. Occasionally, a congregation will assess its major program by comparison with similar programs within other churches. But neither of these halfhearted efforts is adequate.

The standards for, and criteria used to assess, a major program should have integrity that is both comprehensive and critical. Some years ago there was a strong interest on the part of many congregations in developing programs focusing on religious drama. The demise of religious drama in the life of most local churches is directly correlated with the assumption made by many of those churches that because the plays that were offered were religious they did not therefore have to be good drama. Some churches assumed that people would overlook the terribly amateurish quality of the drama because the church was being sincere in its efforts to deal with some religious theme. That whole perspective runs counter to the productive development of competent programs in the life of local congregations.

Should a congregation decide that one of its major programs will be its music program, then it should measure the present stature of its music program by using the critical standards and criteria prevalent in the various music fields in that community. That is, it should measure its music program in comparison to (1) other church music programs, (2) educational music programs, (3) civic music programs, (4) commercial music programs, and (5) general standards for excellence in the field of music prevailing in the community.

The point is simply this: Neither churched people nor unchurched people finally assess their congregation's music program only in relation to other church music programs. Indeed, it is often the case that church people are not very familiar with what is taking place in other church music programs in the community. But it is clearly the case that everyone—both churched and unchurched—experiences music in church, educational, civic, and commercial arenas of life. They tend to assess their own church music program in relation to the experiences of music that they have in day-to-day living.

Communitywide Competence

Generally speaking, a church that has successfully developed a major program that meets that community's standards in that specific field of endeavor earns communitywide respect for that program. Effective congregations tend to have at least one major program that is held in high esteem by the community as a whole. The program may be the music program, the youth program, the mothers' morning out program, a program ministering to aging persons, or a scouting program—the list could go on and on.

Those congregations that develop one such major program become legends on the community grapevine for the quality of work that is shared and accomplished through that major program. Further, that major program tends to draw people from across the community in addition to the congregation's own members. Programs that have this communitywide respect generally have a substantial number of people from the community who either participate in it or in some way share in its support. To put it the other way around, it is seldom the case that any congregation's program will be a major program if it only attracts members and constituents. More often than not, people from the community are attracted to a congregation's program precisely because of the quality of what it shares with those who participate.

Multidimensional Programs

More often than not, a local congregation's major program is multidimensional and focuses on a range of groups and age levels. Most major programs in local churches do not focus on a narrow age range or a select group, although they may have started out that way in their earlier years of development. But they are sufficiently attractive because of their competence that they draw multiple groups and age levels to them.

The multidimensional character of a program creates a dynamic enabling it to become even more fully competent than it has been. That is, as it attracts an increasingly broad range of people from various groups and age levels, it increasingly draws together a more comprehensive and competent range of people who in turn contribute to the growing excellence of the program.

Programs and Leaders

A major program in a local church is generally directed by leaders who make both relational and functional contributions to the program. Indeed, a program tends to become a major program precisely because of this. The leaders have functional competencies in the program area; for example, in a major music program the key leaders bring sound musical training. They further bring sound relational competencies, that is, those that enable them to lead and direct with compassion and good human relations skills. Wherever the combination of relational and functional competencies is well in place, there will be a strong tendency for that program to emerge as one of the major programs in the life of a congregation.

This principle does suggest that it is wise to select leaders who have *both* relational and functional skills for a program the congregation has decided to make one of its major offerings. Regrettably, a vast number of churches select program leaders on the basis of just the functional competencies they bring to their positions. Insufficient attention is given to whether or not the leaders of the program have strong relational competencies as well.

Program and Mission

In addition to the four considerations that have been mentioned, local congregations that could rank themselves 8, 9, or 10 on this central characteristic usually have developed a direct or indirect connection between one of their specific, concrete missional objectives and the major program they have put in place. This is not to say that all programs and activities in the church should have some connection with a missional objective. Nor is it to suggest that every missional objective should have a concomitant program or activity that the church has developed.

Rather, it is simply to indicate that a church is wise to think through the possibility that one of its mission objectives and one of its major programs could supplement and complement the other. This mutual reinforcement would strengthen both. At the same time, such mutual reinforcement should not be artificially contrived. Insofar as it is natural and beneficial, it will be helpful to both that such a connection exists.

The Power of Programs

Spillover

Whenever a church has successfully developed a major program in accordance with the principles we have just discussed, that congregation will benefit from the spillover. This can be seen at two points. First, with one major program well in place, the other programs in that local church tend to rise to its level of competence. And the greater the competence of that major program, the more likely that some of the other programs will rise to that high level of competence. Conversely, if the major program is not done well, this will spill over to lower the level of competence of the other programs and activities in that congregation. The major program sets the standard. The major program sets the level of excellence with which people will be satisfied in a given congregation. If the major program in a congregation is mediocre, probably the other programs and activities will be mediocre or even less. Let a major program set a high standard and the other programs will rise to nearly that level of excellence.

The second spillover effect is seen when people in the community *assume* that the church's other programs offer a comparable degree of excellence. For example, in one church the mothers' morning out program is highly regarded on the grapevine as one of the finest in that community. Families are attracted to the quality of that specific program. Some of those families have visited the service of worship again and again because of their assumption that the service of worship would be likely to have the same quality as the mothers' morning out program.

The community's impression of a congregation's total program is largely formed by their perception of the major programs for which that congregation is known in the community.

Four to Five Years

Whenever a congregation intentionally decides to develop a specific major program, it is important that that local congregation plan on four to five years of development. It takes a considerable investment of leadership, time, and money to put in place the quality and caliber of major programs that are found in effective, successful congregations.

It often happens that the congregation chooses a given program to become one of its major program offerings but makes the mistake of rushing hurriedly to put it into place. They use a crisis orientation in the development of its foundations. They make hurried decisions on leadership, time, and money. They make the disastrous assumption that the more committed they are to developing it, the more likely it is to become a major program. A year or two later they wonder why it hasn't happened. In about the second or third year they pull back their leadership, their time, and their money, and they watch the program fail.

The program fails to become a major program because of "quick closure." That is, the leaders of the congregation are looking for a quick way to achieve a major program in a given area of the life of that church. They want an immediate achievement. Typical examples of this are youth programs, music programs, recreational programs, and programs with homebound persons. Generally, they develop a crash approach in the hope that they will be delivering a competent program almost overnight. When they begin to sense that that has not happened and is not going to happen, they become disappointed and depressed; they slacken the investment of leadership, time, and financial resources; finally they lose heart and then wonder why such a worthwhile program failed to meet their expectations.

It takes four to five years to develop and build any program into a major program in the life of a church and a community. It takes five or more years to develop a professional football team into being a winning, pro team. If it takes that long to develop winning competencies in something finally as simple as professional football, it is not surprising that it takes at least four to five years to develop a major program to help people with their complex hurts and hopes, plans and directions, disappointments and accomplishments in life's pilgrimage on earth.

Programs and Merry-Go-Rounds

Too many churches are merry-go-rounds of programs and activities, and not enough churches are mission posts of help and hope. Too many congregations have bought into the idea that the purpose of the church is to provide programs and activities for all ages and all people. It takes some churches the better part of a full page to list all the programs and activities offered. Indeed, pastors and church leaders become so busily involved in spinning that merry-go-round of programs and activities faster and faster that they have hardly any time left to participate in the church's mission in the world.

The implicit assumption is that of a Bo-Peep church, namely, the congregation is implicitly stating to the community that it will offer a wide range of programs and activities to interest people in coming. Basically, it takes the stance of passively waiting for unchurched people to participate in the smorgasbord of programs and activities that it offers. Committee meetings, planning sessions, programs, and activities prevent people from being genuinely and authentically involved in mission in the community.

To some extent this excessive investment of leadership time and money in the programs and activities of local congregations can be attributed to the desire for safety and security. That is, it is safer and more secure to invest one's leadership, time, and money in the quiet and safety of programs and activities inside a local church than it is to seek out lost people in rough, rocky places of life and share with them help and hope. Because of the factors of safety and security, there may always be more Bo-Peep Christians in a given local church than there are Good Shepherd Christians. Even Bo-Peep Christians will better serve God's kingdom as they focus on developing one or two or three major programs rather than a merry-go-round of programs spinning faster and faster until the life and mission of the church becomes a blur of pretty colors and people are lost because of preoccupation with programs.

Programs and Hope

Having shared such a dismal portrait of programs and activities, the reader might assume that what will follow is a statement of hope; the reader will be moderately misguided in making that assumption. Regrettably, the more a given congregation loses members, the more it seems to invest increasing amounts of leadership time and financial resources in more and more programs. It is as if local congregations seek to recover the busy, bustling days of programs and activities of the churched culture of the 1950s. Those days are gone and done. We look forward to the 1980s.

The hope for congregations who seek to be effective and successful in the unchurched culture of the 1980s is to focus on people, not programs. It is to focus on mission and visitation, to share worship and groups. The hope of these congregations is in developing leadership resources and solid participatory decision making; only then—after all these strengths are reasonably well in place—might it make sense to invest leadership, time, and money in programs and activities.

The hope for churches in the 1980s is not in program development and coordination, but in carrying out a few programs so well that these few programs develop communitywide respect for the competence and caring shared through them. The key to program development and program coordination in the future is to work smarter, not harder—that is, to do a few things well. Quit seeking to offer everything and anything to everybody all the time.

When a congregation does focus on just a few programs and does them so extraordinarily well that the community is enriched, then that congregation will become increasingly effective and successful. Moreover, it will see the value of programs as nurturing the gifts, talents, strengths, and competence of people. That congregation will have put away the foolish notion still persistent in a few churches that programs are ends in themselves. To be sure, no church would admit that some of its programs have become ends in themselves. But again and again, unchurched persons in the community will be able to tell whether the purpose of the program is a program, not people. An effective congregation is one that has one or two or three such programs so well in place that *people* are helped and hope is shared.

Rating Guide: Several Competent Programs and Activities

Item	Maximum Points	Your Church's Rating
1. To what extent does the local church have comprehensive and critical criteria for evaluating its programs?	25	_____
2. Does the local church have from 1 to 3 programs that are respected for their community-wide competence?	25	_____
3. To what extent are those programs substantially multidimensional in terms of the groups and age levels they reach?	15	_____
4. To what degree are the leaders of those programs both relational and functional in their leadership?	15	_____
5. Is there a close relationship between those programs and the key missional objectives of the local church?	20	_____
Total:	100	_____

INSTRUCTIONS:

- Use the information in the chapter as a resource in evaluating your church's rating in each of the listed items.
- Enter the rating numbers in the blanks and then find the total.
- Divide the total of your assessment score by 10 to obtain your church's rating on a scale of 1 to 10.
- Enter that rating on the rating scale for Several Competent Programs and Activities in Figure C.1.

8. Open Accessibility

Location Is Decisive

The eighth central characteristic that many effective, successful congregations have well in place as an 8, 9 or 10 is open accessibility. This characteristic and the ninth central characteristic—high visibility—are closely related. To a large extent, accessibility and visibility are almost inseparable characteristics. At the same time, it is possible to focus separately on each of them in an accurate analysis of the current strengths of a given local church. Accessibility is slightly more important than visibility as a central characteristic of effective, successful churches.

Accessibility consists of location accessibility, sight accessibility and people accessibility. In large measure, location is decisive. In real estate development circles, the basic principle is reiterated as follows: Three factors are important in developing a successful business. The first factor is location, the second factor is location, the third factor is location. Based on my experience in consultation, location is just as decisive in the development of an effective, successful local church, followed by sight accessibility, then, people accessibility.

Accessibility and Openness

Location Accessibility

Three factors affect the location accessibility of a church site. The first of these is traffic direction pattern—the routes people travel going to work or shopping. The best site for a church is one on the major traffic direction pattern within the area the church plans to serve, preferably on a corner adjacent to major north-south and east-west traffic arteries. The larger the area a church plans to serve, the more important it is that it be located on more than one major traffic direction pattern. The church that is on only one major traffic direction pattern is at a disadvantage compared with the church located adjacent to two or three.

It is important, in conjunction with this principle, that the site be such that the traffic direction patterns bring people toward it. For example, if people travel to the south or west going to work or shopping, the best site would be one sufficiently south or west that people would find it natural to travel to that location, since it is concurrent with their traffic direction patterns in day-to-day life. In that community, the location accessibility of a site to the north or east would not be as good. That is, people are less likely to travel to a church site that is not located in harmony with their normal traffic direction patterns.

The second factor in location accessibility is average trip time. The best site is one that takes seriously the average trip time in the community. Every community has dominant patterns of average trip time. In some communities the average trip time is twenty-five minutes. In other communities the average trip time is fifteen minutes. It is also important to evaluate travel time to a church site in relation to average trip time, insofar as it can be projected reasonably, during the coming ten years. In some instances, churches may benefit from the fact that over the coming ten years the average trip time in a particular commuity is growing longer.

Generally speaking, people tend to invest approximately the same amount of time traveling to church that they invest in an average trip during the course of the week—an average trip to work, to do major shopping, or to participate in social and recreational activities.

The third factor in location accessibility is the sense of openness the site presents to the people who see it. The more spacious and open it seems, the more likely people are to sense that site as accessible. The more closed in and cluttered it seems, the more likely people are to sense inaccessibility. Landscaping that communicates openness and beauty improves the sense of accessibility. A site that has large buildings on either side built clear to the street will seem less open and less accessible than a site where the adjacent buildings are set back from the road with sufficient green space surrounding them. The interrelationship of land use, landscaping, and architectural design should be a consideration in evaluating the location accessibility of any church. To be sure, the sense of openness is an intangible factor. One almost has to see the site and the surrounding area to be able to discern whether or not that site connotes accessibility.

Site Accessibility

Three factors contribute to site accessibility. The first of these has to do with entering and leaving the property. The basic principle is the larger the site, the more important it is to have multiple entrances and exits. The smaller the site, the easier it is to get by with only one or two. A common mistake is that of selecting a large piece of property and then providing only one major point for entering and leaving that property. Such an arrangement seriously damages the site accessibility.

It should be observed that entrances and exits to the property are best designed for two-way traffic at each point; one-way entrances and exits are less desirable. Indeed, in larger sites it may be important to have available three traffic lanes at each. Clearly, this is dependent on the size of the traffic flow on Sunday mornings and on whether the church has more than one service of worship (which generates the problem of some people leaving the first service even as others are coming to the second). The second factor in site accessibility is that of entrances and exits to the buildings. Regrettably, too few churches have built facilities with adequate attention to this. A building that has entrances with large vestibule areas at the major entrances and exits meets this criterion. Site accessibility also calls for adequate provision for handicapped persons. The third factor is that of "hidden signs"—signs that communicate a sense of warmth, a sense of openness and accessibility, and a sense of welcome and invitation. Do visitors to your church feel welcomed by what they see—or do the hidden signs flash Proceed with Caution? For example, some churches hang out the hidden sign Handicapped Persons Unwelcome. Still others suggest, Guess Where the Sanctuary Is; We Know, But We Aren't Telling. A substantial number of churches hang out the hidden sign, We Know Where the Parking Is; We've Claimed Our Parking Spaces; You Figure Out What to Do. The location may indeed be accessible, but if the congregation hangs out enough hidden signs that communicate inaccessibility people will immediately conclude that the location, the buildings, and the congregation are inaccessible.

People Accessibility

Unchurched persons primarily discern the warmth of a whole congregation by their contacts with individual people in that congregation. The third principal factor in open accessibility is that of people accessibility. To be sure, location accessibility and site accessibility are more tangible and measurable than the factor of people accessibility. At the same, it *is* possible to assess with some degree of reliability how much people accessibility there is within a congregation. People accessibility means the pastor and key leaders of the congregation are accessible to individuals in the congregation, to the general community, and to those whom that church is serving in intentional, missional ways.

There are a range of simple clues that will suggest the extent to which the pastor and the key leaders are accessible to members of the congregation. Does the pastor have an open-door policy? Do key leaders have closed, secret meetings or open, invitational meetings? Do the pastor and key leaders invest considerable amounts of time in informal discussion and conversation with members of the congregation? Sometimes, a pastor and key leaders will schedule themselves so busily with meetings and projects that there is not sufficient open time for them to share in informal conversations with the people in the congregation. The ease with which the pastor can be reached in times of emergency, illness, and death will give a further clue as to how much people accessibility there is.

Accessibility to the community in general can be discovered fairly straightforwardly by gaining some sense of whether or not the pastor and the leaders of the church participate individually and readily in community activities. The more they contribute to activities within the community, the more likely people in the community are to feel that this church has strong people accessibility. The more the pastor and key leaders stay within the safety of their congregation's space and facilities, the less likely the community at large is to feel that that congregation is accessible.

The community grapevine will spread the word about a congregation's people accessibility if the pastor and the leaders of the church are accessible to persons whom the church is seeking to serve in specific, concrete, missional ways. Regrettably, some pastors and lay leaders seek to be in mission through programs and community agencies without having direct contact with the individuals served. It is important to be aware that the people within the congregation, the community, and the missional arenas of the church draw fairly strong conclusions as to whether or not a given pastor and key leaders have people accessibility, and though this may be comparatively intangible, it is nevertheless something about which people develop definite impressions and conclusions.

Overcoming Shortcomings

Visitation

If a given congregation has neither location accessibility nor site accessibility, one way it can compensate for lack of open accessibility is to develop an increasingly strong program of pastoral and lay visitation. The less accessible the site is, the more important it becomes for the pastor and lay persons to be accessible in people's homes and places of work.

In an unchurched culture, pastoral and lay visitation is extraordinarily important in its own right. Indeed, it is the second most important of the twelve characteristics present in effective, successful churches. Whenever accessibility in terms of location and site is not present, the characteristic of pastoral and lay visitation becomes even more crucial in developing the future and destiny of the congregation. Should accessibility be rated as 4 on a scale of 1 to 10, it would be important for pastoral and lay visitation to be 10. That is, it would not be sufficient to do pastoral and lay visitation of less than the highest level. We can compensate for a lack of accessibility by engaging in a substantial program of pastoral and lay visitation.

With an extraordinarily good program of visitation, a local congregation is able to counter and overcome a lack of location and site accessibility by creating a strong sense of people accessibility. This may be a *result* of visitation—but it should not be confused with the *goal* of visitation.

Mission

There are ways other than pastoral and lay visitation of compensating for the lack of accessibility. A congregation could have a service of worship that is so corporate and dynamic in character that it communicates a sense of accessibility. A congregation may develop an extensive network of significant relational groups in the community, as well as in the church, creating another avenue of accessibility.

But let me speak of mission. A congregation may deliver such effective mission to a specific human need that it becomes a legend on the community grapevine for its accessibility to people. One congregation with which I have worked had developed an extraordinary missional outreach with alcoholics and their families. Indeed, that particular congregation has delivered one of the most competent and effective missional approaches with alcoholics and their families in the country. It became a legend on the community grapevine for its accessibility to people. It became known as a church where someone could contact a pastor or lay leader day or night and receive direct help and assistance. It became a church where persons discovered that the pastor and key lay leaders spent enormous amounts of time in the community helping people with their hurts and hopes. To that extent, the church overcame its location and site inaccessibility by having extraordinarily good people accessibility through its specific, concrete, missional objective of serving alcoholics and their families.

Conclusion

During the coming years, accessibility will become increasingly important. The more crowded and cluttered our towns and cities become, the more important accessibility is. The more complex and difficult our lives become, the more important that churches be accessible and open. Indeed, it will become important that congregations evidence an intentional, aggressive accessibility. New congregations, as well as existing congregations, would do well to evaluate their location accessibility, their site accessibility, and their people accessibility and to put in place a substantive plan to improve accessibility of the congregation in all three arenas. Clearly, I would encourage congregations to look seriously at visitation and mission as ways of improving and enhancing open accessibility.

Rating Guide: Open Accessibility

Item	Maximum Points	Your Church's Rating
1. How good is location accessibility?	40	_____
2. Site accessibility?	20	_____
3. People accessibility?	40	_____
Total:	100	_____

INSTRUCTIONS:

- Use the information in the chapter as a resource in evaluating your church's rating in each of the listed items.
- Enter the rating numbers in the blanks and then find the total.
- Divide the total of your assessment score by 10 to obtain your church's rating on a scale of 1 to 10.
- Enter that rating on the rating scale for Open Accessibility in Figure C.1.

9. High Visibility

Accessibility and Visibility

The ideal combination is for a local church to have both visibility and accessibility. These two strengths significantly reinforce one another in ways that are beneficial to the congregation. Some churches will have accessibility and virtually no visibility. Other congregations will have high visibility but suffer a lack of accessibility. Wherever possible, it is helpful for the local church to have both characteristics well in place.

There is high visibility when a local congregation has developed the geographical visibility of its site, community visibility with regard to its pastor, key leaders, and major programs, and media visibility in the communications networks that exist in its community. It is useful for a local congregation to be highly visible in all three arenas.

Seeing the Church

The Physical Visibility of the Church Site

It is quite straightforward. Either the church can be seen or it cannot be seen. That is, either the physical site can be seen by persons in the community or its visibility is marginal. You can determine the physical visibility of a given church site by answering the following three questions:

1. Can the church site be easily seen from major traffic arteries?
2. How many people in fact see the church site each day?
3. How many people see the church site in a given week?

It is obvious that the more people who see a given church site, the more likely some of them are to think of that church site as a possible source of help.

Now, the key to this has to do with whether or not people "really see" the church site. It is not at all uncommon for major buildings to recede into the background in such a fashion that people hardly even notice they are there. They become, if you will, virtually invisible. Church sites that remain essentially the same from one year to the next have a strong tendency to recede into the background. New people hardly notice them; unchurched persons get used to "not seeing" them. Churches that fail to add "points of interest" to their landscaping from one year to the next tend to become anonymous buildings that people pass by but do not really see. Shrubbery and trees that are allowed to grow so tall and bushy that they interfere with the essential view of the site and the buildings also contribute to the church becoming increasingly invisible as time passes.

Another factor related to physical visibility is that of "high side" visibility. For example, if a committee were searching for a location for a new church, they would be best advised to purchase a piece of property that is on the high side of the major roads adjacent to the property. Churches that are "down in the gulley" are virtually invisible. It may be one thing to *sing* about the church in the valley, but it is quite another thing for churches to be located on the low side of the road to the extent that they are hardly ever noticed.

Regrettably, many church location committees settle for a piece of property on the low side of the road because they think it will be cheaper. To be sure, the initial cost of the property is less; it is precisely because it is on the low side of the road that it costs so much less. But the price that is paid over the coming forty to sixty to a hundred years of that congregation's existence is not worth the initial savings. High-side visibility is important to the physical visibility of the site.

Yet another factor related to physical visibility is the amount of frontage on the road or roads adjacent to the property. Again, church location committees frequently select the site that may contain as much as five to seven acres but with a frontage on the major road or roads of no more than fifty to a hundred feet. The narrower the frontage, the less visible the site will be, no matter how many acres it may contain. Physical visibility is enhanced by extensive frontage on the principle roads adjacent to the property.

Community Visibility

Community visibility is equally as important as physical visibility. Indeed, the less the physical visibility of the site, the *more* important it is that there should be high community visibility. Obviously, this point is directly connected to the earlier point concerning open accessibility. Community visibility is of two types: (1) public visibility and (2) grapevine visibility.

Public visibility is the extent to which the pastor and key leaders of the congregation have reasonably high visibility in the community. High visibility is developed as they participate in the broad range of community activities in the area that the church serves. The extent to which the church is involved in community activities, and the extent to which people in the community recognize the pastor and key leaders of the congregation and their work in the church and the community is the extent to which the local church has public visibility. Simply put, public visibility has to do with whether or not the pastor and key leaders of the church are seen and recognized in the life and activities of the community.

The second type of community visibility is grapevine visibility, and it is as important, if not more important, than public visibility. In every community there is an informal network of relationships among its people and groups. Communication travels along this grapevine network as rapidly as it does on radio or television. In many communities the informal networks of conversation and communication are the primary sources that people depend upon for information about what is really happening in their area.

Grapevine visibility means that a given local church has nurtured on the community grapevine a good feeling about its life and work. There is a sense in which the church, by its effective mission, has created a solid image of helping people. The pastor and key leaders of a local church can even virtually become living legends on the community grapevine. When that happens, a local church has an extraordinarily high degree of community visibility.

It should be observed that the important factor in both public and grapevine visibility is the character and content of what is communicated. Churches that have a useful community visibility tend to have the kind of visibility that identifies that church as a source of help and hope and as a source of reliability and certainty amidst the difficulties and transitions of everyday life. That is, it is very important that a local congregation *not* develop a grapevine visibility that suggests the pastor or lay leaders of that congregation are "con artists" or are interested primarily in "gimmicks and gadgets" that focus on faddish programs and activities. The substance of the visibility is decisive. It is to be hoped that a local congregation will reflect upon the impression and image that it has created in both its public and its grapevine visibility. Not all churches create the impression and image that they have intended.

Now, this does not suggest that a church should develop a preoccupation with community visibility. Rather, it is to suggest that every local congregation has some community visibility whether it wants it or not. Whether it be two women visiting with one another at the grocery store or two men in conversation in a field or on a street corner, those persons, insofar as they discuss a local church, discuss their present impressions of that church. People in the community do develop an impression as to whether a given local church is sincere in its commitment to help people in the name and power of Christ, or whether it is primarily interested in using those people for some purpose. As you well know, the word spreads fast—one way or the other.

Media Visibility

Whether it be newspapers, radio, television, or other forms of media, the extent to which a local church advances its visibility through the media that are available, is the extent to which that local congregation contributes to high visibility. Jesus said, "Let your light so shine before people, that they may see your good works and give glory to your Father who is in heaven."

Frequently, churches feel uncomfortable about media visibility and public relations. They sometimes fear that developing media and public relations visibility is too much akin to "blowing your own horn" and therefore is something in which the church should not be involved. What we must realize is that every group or organization, to a greater or lesser extent, is discussed in whatever media are present in that community. It would be most unusual for a year to go by without the media making some reference, however obliquely, to a given local congregation and its life and work. To be sure, churches in major metropolitan areas are less likely to receive media attention. But in towns and rural areas churches are frequently referred to by the media. Media visibility and public relations should not be ignored. In churches that rank as 8, 9, or 10 on the central characteristic of high visibility, one will frequently find that a solid public relations program is well in place.

Three facts about public relations are fundamental to understanding media visibility. First, the basic element is integrity; without integrity there can be no substantive public relations effort. Indeed, without integrity it would be wise not to have community visibility—if you could avoid it. People are reasonably astute at discerning an "advertising campaign" that does not have substance or strength derived from the fundamental life and mission of a church. Some churches have tried to convince the public that they are solidly engaged in mission when, in fact, all they are engaged in is trying to convince the public that they are. Eventually this lack of integrity will be found out. Thus, whenever a church enters the field of media visibility it is important that that church share honestly what it is doing and planning to do in mission in the community. Such an approach must have about it a thoughtful integrity.

The second fact about public relations and media visibility has to do with the focus of the public relations program. Some local churches have focused on what people can do for that church if only those people will come and participate in that church's programs and activities. Some churches have focused on high-powered promises of what that church can do for them if those people will only become participants in the life of that congregation.

Media visibility and public relations cannot be a kind of chocolate syrup poured over flavorless ice cream to make it taste sweet. Most people are not interested in overstatement about what a congregation is doing. Most people respect a local church whenever it shares what it is doing and what it is planning to do as it lives out the gospel. Not all people are interested in which speaker is coming, or which singing group; they are interested in knowing what the church is doing to be of help in the community so that it will be a better place in which to live.

The third fact about media visibility has to do with the mutual trust that a local church develops with the media agencies in the community. Even when there is an awkward situation in a local church, the pastor or key leaders should be thoughtfully honest and forthright, giving the facts as accurately as possible. Chances are that awkward situations will be reported anyway. Candor and openness will create a better relationship of mutual trust and respect. That relationship will stand the church in good stead on a long-term basis as it works to put in place a rightful and appropriate degree of media visibility.

Points of Interest, Signs, and People

Points of Interest

The physical visibility of a church site can be substantially improved as that church develops modest "points of interest" in the landscaping around the church. It is most worthwhile for a local church to change one or two points of interest each year so as to help people see the site in new and fresh ways. Too many churches leave their landscaping essentially the same year in and year out. I am not suggesting that the church do major landscape revisions each year. Nor am I suggesting that the church overhaul its total landscaping over a three to five year period. Rather, I do suggest that the church select one or two points of interest— generally, in the front yard area—and make creative changes from one year to the next in those one or two spots.

For example, near the church sign in the front yard a modest flower bed might create a point of interest. It would be helpful for the size and shape and color of those flowers to be revised from one year to the next. Indeed, it may be useful to move the spot from time to time. Usually, the creation of such points of interest can be done inexpensively and easily. It is hard for the pastor and leaders of the congregation to see the church site the way it is seen by unchurched people and by others in the community. It is amazing the number of pastors and leaders who mistakenly assume that the way they see the church site is the way everyone sees it. Their own familiarity with the church gets in the way of their coming to grips with the fact that numbers of people may not even "see" the physical site of the church at all. Modest points of interest will help catch the attention of those in the community who might have some eventual interest in that congregation.

Signs

Most church signs are foolishly done. They carry too much information; they are located in the wrong position in relation to the traffic direction patterns on the adjacent roads; and they are allowed to become worn and weather-beaten and, therefore, to communicate the sense that this might be a declining congregation.

Church signs should be two- or three-second signs. That is, given the speed of the traffic that passes a church, there should be only as much information on the sign as a driver can read in two to three seconds. The five-second sign has too much information on it; the driver will not read even part of such a sign. The driver glances at a sign, sees that it has too much information on it, and absorbs none of it.

The sign should simply state one or two key facts that the church wishes to communicate. For example, the sign might share simply and straightforwardly the name of the church and the name of the pastor. The name of the pastor should not be hung on a separate temporary sign underneath the real sign. Both the church's name and the pastor's name should communicate a sense of stability and reliability, a sense of permanence and presence.

It may be that the church would also want to add the time of the major service of worship. But, signs that communicate the name of the church, the name of the pastor, the time of the first service of worship, the time of Sunday school, the time of the second service of worship, the time of the youth fellowship, and the time of the Wednesday evening program have so much information that hardly any of it will be seen by unchurched persons. Such signs come across as cluttered and crowded, and drivers have more important things to do—like keeping their cars on the road—than to try and read through all of that.

Further, signs do not need to say visitors are welcome. The shape of the sign, the position of the sign, the colors used for background, and the lettering will all communicate a sense of warmth and welcome. It does not need to be also stated on the sign itself. A nearby "point of interest" such as a patch of flowers that have beauty and warmth will communicate the sense of openness and invitation that it is important to communicate.

More often than not, signs that are exactly parallel or exactly perpendicular to the road are not as easily seen as signs that are at some angle to oncoming traffic. That means that frequently a church will need two signs. One sign will be located in such a way that those coming, for example, from east to west will see it in sufficient time to read the important information on it. That church will have another sign located at an appropriate angle for those coming from west to east to see. The general principle is that the faster the average speed of the traffic, the more important it is to have an adequate line of sight so that drivers can read the sign from some distance away rather than being expected to catch the sign at the very point at which they are passing both the sign and the church itself.

To be sure, I would advocate that signs be tastefully and aesthetically designed. I would not in any way suggest flashing neon signs or huge, glaring billboards. At the same time, the only reason for devoting so much detail to this point is that in my travels across the country as a consultant, I have seen the variety of mistakes congregations make on something as simple as a sign. Adequate signs will contribute to high visibility.

People

The best signs are finally people. People point people to a church. People who are visible in helping people contribute to the high visibility of a congregation. Mostly, these people are quiet and modest. Mostly, they are shy of publicity and do their helping and missional work with the hope that their help will be effective. They do not want publicity and they do not want their work to be ballyhooed abroad.

These people are the saints in the church. They are the persons who have visibility as being significantly helpful in the lives of people. The more helping persons the congregation has at work in the community, not in the church, the more that congregation will have high visibility in the community. The power of people is necessary and important in order for a local church to have high visibility as one of its central strengths and characteristics.

Rating Guide: High Visibility

Item	Maximum Points	Your Church's Rating
1. How good is the physical visibility of your church?	40	_____
2. Its community visibility?	30	_____
3. Its media visibility?	30	_____
Total:	100	_____

INSTRUCTIONS:

- Use the information in the chapter as a resource in evaluating your church's rating in each of the listed items.
- Enter the rating numbers in the blanks and then find the total.
- Divide the total of your assessment score by 10 to obtain your church's rating on a scale of 1 to 10.
- Enter that rating on the rating scale for High Visibility in Figure C.1.

10. Adequate Parking, Land, and Landscaping

Parking and Participation

Parking, land, and landscaping are interrelated factors that contribute to participation. Obviously, the amount of land available to a congregation determines the number of parking spaces that congregation can make available to persons who wish to participate. Further, the amount of land in relation to that portion committed to parking usually determines the amount of land that may be designated for landscaping purposes.

Parking is a decisive factor in the life of a congregation. There is a direct correlation between parking and participation. The more adequate the parking, the more likely there is to be strong participation in church school and worship.

Moreover, there is a direct correlation between participation and giving. Indeed, there is a correlation between parking and worship attendance and a further correlation between worship attendance and giving. The church that is short on parking may very well be short on worship attendance and, therefore, on contributions. People who participate in a congregation tend to contribute to that congregation. People who are members of the congregation but who do not participate tend not to contribute financially. Parking, land, and landscaping are more important than many pastors and leaders of congregations have thought.

Parking and People

Parking

Mostly, local congregations have available two kinds of parking: (1) on-street parking and (2) off-street parking. With regard to on-street parking, each local congregation will have to make a reasonable judgment as to how many parking spaces are actually available to that church on-street on those occasions when it has major programs and activities.

Some churches make the mistake of counting *all* the on-street parking spaces as though they would automatically be available to that church especially on Sunday morning. Such is frequently not the case. Residents may park on the street. Persons who participate in other nearby congregations may park on the street. Shoppers in a nearby business may use on-street parking spaces. Roughly speaking, I have found that a local church is fortunate to be able to count on 50–60 percent of the total on-street parking spaces for its use on Sunday mornings. Certainly, there are scattered exceptions to this across the country. At the same time, the basic point is to be realistic as to the number of on-street spaces available.

In a similar fashion, it is important for the pastor and lay leaders of the congregation to be realistic as to the number of off-street parking spaces available. I have used the term "off-street" rather than the term "on-site" because many churches depend upon off-street parking that is really not on the church site. For example, in a town that is a county seat, the local congregation depended on the off-street parking available at an adjacent bank. Generally, various businesses are quite willing for a local church to use their off-street parking on Sunday morning. Even if this is the case, it will be useful for the long-range plan of the local church to ask seriously for how many years they can depend upon these nearby businesses to make available their own off-street parking.

The most effective parking is within one block of the church. Therefore, it is important that both on-street and off-street parking be within one short walking block of the major space and facilities of the local church. Parking within a second block is less usable and desirable. Parking three blocks away can be virtually written off in most situations.

A case in point is to illustrate behavior patterns when people go to local shopping centers. Some individuals are three-minute individuals. That is, they will invest three minutes of their time driving around the parking area looking for the space right next to the door so they will not have to walk very far. Some people are five-minute individuals. They will invest approximately five minutes in such a search. I even know of persons who will follow someone who is leaving the store with packages in the hopes that they will go to a car at one of the immediately adjacent spaces and drive away, thereby opening that parking space near the door.

Many local congregations are unrealistic about the amount of parking they really have. First, they generally do not know the number of parking spaces they have. Second, they are generally unrealistic as to the number of on-street parking spaces they can count on Sunday after Sunday. Further, they tend not to be realistic about the number of off-street spaces available. To make matters even worse, local congregations tend not to take seriously enough the limiting factor that optimal parking is within the first short walking block.

An average ratio of parking spaces to people is 1 to 1.75; that is, each car brings an average of 1.75 people. In some parts of the country the average may be as high as 2.25 persons per car, and yet in other parts of the country the ratio may be as high as 2.5 persons per car. Frequently,

Figure 10.1   Church Parking Formula

a. Develop a site plan to show the location of the principal buildings and the on-street and off-street parking.

b. Compute the church parking formula

1. Number of on-street parking spaces within reasonable walking distance (1–2 blocks) of church. _____

2. If applicable, reduce the on-street parking figure by 50% to ascertain likely available parking. _____

3. Number of off-street parking spaces within reasonable walking distance (1–2 blocks) of church. _____

   Note: Count only the first and second floors of decked parking

4. Add the figures in 2 and 3 to ascertain total available church parking. _____

5. Multiply total parking spaces by 1.75 to ascertain total number of people for whom the church provides parking. _____

6. Divide total parking spaces figure into total church income per year to discover "annual value" of each parking space. _____

a family of five will drive two cars. When one of the children becomes a teenager, they may even bring three cars.

The simplest way to discover the ratio for your own church's parking is to count the total number of persons who are present on a given hour on Sunday morning and then to count the number of cars that are parked on-street and off-street by those who are participating that hour. It would be best to do this analytical exercise on at least five Sundays to get a sufficient data base to track out an accurate ratio of persons to parking spaces. Basically, the point is that a local congregation that has 100 parking spaces (some on-street and some off-street) will have approximately 175 persons in worship on a given Sunday.

Two further points need to be mentioned. First, in rural areas a person driving by a local church might assume that the people who are parked around that church do not know how to park. That is, cars are frequently scattered in an interesting hodgepodge. No discernable parking areas are identified. In point of fact, often the hodgepodge character of the parking is really quite straightforward and useful. That is, people park under the shade trees in the summer. During the winter they simply continue to park in those same areas.

The second point has to do with the "hidden sign" in front of the church. Some researchers suggest that it is important for a church to have approximately 20 percent of its parking area empty on a given Sunday so that the large hidden sign that is hung out front says "come on in; there is room in the inn for you." The further point is made that when the parking is full it has the same net effect as a sanctuary that is uncomfortably crowded. That is, when the parking lot or lots are full, the big hidden sign hung out front is "there is no room in this inn for you."

In actual practice, the pastor and key leaders frequently arrive early on Sunday morning. They invest much of their Sunday morning inside the church building. More often than not, they have little knowledge of the parking realities at their particular church. Indeed, they may not have much appreciation of how important parking is to participation.

The chart in Figure 10.1 will help you calculate the number of parking spaces and number of persons who are thereby able to participate. From that information, you will also be able to develop some estimate of the income per year in relation to the number of parking spaces available.

Land

There is considerable debate in church extension committees about the amount of land it is useful and helpful for a local congregation to own. Were we considering starting new congregations in metropolitan areas, I would recommend, more often than not, that the new site contain five to seven acres of land. Were we giving consideration to starting a new congregation in a rural area, I would recommend three to eight acres—depending on the long-term usage the congregation envisions for its property.

The size of a local church's property significantly influences the number of buildings, the number of parking spaces, and the amount of landscaping that can be placed on that church site. Churches tend to lack sufficient land space for their total life and mission. Frequently, the church will be given a piece of land. The church is grateful for the contribution, but at the time, they do not assess clearly enough all the ways in which they might want to utilize that piece of land. Hence, over the years, they slowly discover that the original piece of land they acquired is not adequate.

Further, many congregations pass up solid opportunities to acquire additional adjacent land; often, they decide that the asking price for it is too high. They remember when that land was worth only $1,000 an acre and now someone has the audacity to be asking $1,500 an acre for the land. With that kind of attitude, the people negotiating the purchase of the land on behalf of the church tend to try and get a "bargain." The result is that they offend the owner of the adjacent property and lose the opportunity for some years to come to have meaningful conversations about the purchase of that property.

Two other factors are important in relation to a local congregation's land. These are the shape of the land and the contour of the land. The best shape for a church site location is either a rectangle or a square. Oblong rectangles or unusually shaped triangles of land do not make good sense. It becomes very difficult to put the needed kinds of facilities, as well as parking and adequate landscaping, on that shape of property.

A key factor in the contour of most pieces of property is adequate water drainage in relation to the buildings, the related parking areas, and the landscaping areas. Contour and drainage must be taken into account when planning placement of buildings and parking so that drainage problems can be corrected before buildings are built. Otherwise, churches may find themselves faced with building repairs from damage due to water seeping into the lower floors.

Landscaping

In the discussion of high visibility, I pointed out the value of "points of interest" in the overall landscaping plan. There is no need to repeat that material here. Two related points do, however, need to be made about landscaping. The first is that landscaping frequently contributes greatly to a sense of welcome and invitation and a spirit of openness and spaciousness.

Passersby do form their impression of the congregation with what they see as they drive by. Should they see essentially crowded and cluttered landscaping, they are likely to conclude that this church is not for them. "You never get a second chance to make a first impression." Many churches do not realize the kind of first impression they make with unchurched individuals, as well as their own church members, simply by the way in which the landscaping communicates.

The second observation about landscaping is about using some green areas for parking purposes; that is, in many parts of the country, the climate is such that cars can be parked on grass once a week and the grass will continue to be an attractive green area for aesthetic and recreational purposes throughout the rest of the week. One does not need to pour asphalt on all the grass surrounding the church. Indeed, that would be a terrible mistake in terms of both aesthetics and parking.

There is absolutely nothing wrong with people being encouraged to park on certain grass areas that also serve as play areas during the week. This makes it possible to have the best of two worlds: There is available a green space through the week that is used secondarily on Sunday morning for parking. This would be an excellent way to go in many parts of the country for 30–40 percent of the total parking that a congregation needs.

Parking and Long Term Investments

Parking Supervisors

As has been discussed earlier, one way to ease the parking problem in a given church is to establish a team of parking supervisors who facilitate traffic flow and extend help to people as they seek places to park. This constitutes a major way to improve parking at a given church.

Generally, it is important to ask someone to serve as a parking supervisor who has a warm personality and some human relation skills. Parking supervisors should appear to be trustworthy, reliable sources of help. They should take seriously the traffic flow patterns and make it easier for individuals to enter and leave the church site.

Multiple Services

In some instances, the parking is no longer adequate for the congregation. Should that have happened in your church, one idea to consider would be changing to multiple worship services. Now, that does not double the amount of parking that the church might have available, but it would certainly advance the parking considerably beyond what is now available.

Having multiple services might mean that at 9:30 A.M. there is both church school and morning worship; it might also be that both worship and church school are available again at 11:00 A.M. In this book, it is not important to get caught up in detailed analysis of which would be best. The basic point is simply that one can stretch limited parking by providing multiple services.

Visitation, Worship, and Groups

It is possible for a local church to overcome inadequate parking, land, and landscaping by developing even more effective strengths in visitation, worship, and groups. People are sometimes willing to put up with a poor parking situation because of the visitation that they have received in their homes and places of work, because of the corporate and dynamic character of the worship service, and because they have discovered their place in a group that shares with them significant relationships of help and hope.

Again, when a functional characteristic like parking is weak, it can frequently be overcome by building strengths in such relational characteristics as visitation, worship, and groups.

Investment in Relation to Return

Where a congregation is considering the purchase of additional property for parking and landscaping, that congregation frequently thinks in terms of how much the parcel of land costs. That is an inadequate way of factoring the expense of a piece of property. A cost-effective approach would be to calculate the amount of income that is likely to be received per parking space during the coming five to ten years.

A responsible, cost-effective approach would be to discover the total income currently being generated in relation to the number of parking spaces the church now has. Do this by taking the total giving for a year and dividing that figure by the number of parking spaces available. That will yield an average income per year per parking space. Then, multiply that average income per year per parking space by the number of new parking spaces that would be available on the land that the church hopes to purchase. If the cost of the land is less than the net new income that is likely to come to the church during the coming five to ten years, then the purchase of that land for parking constitutes a solid, cost-effective decision.

For example, in a given situation, suppose the adjacent piece of property had a selling price of $50,000 dollars. By research and analysis, it was determined that it would be possible to place 100 parking spaces on that piece of land. Further analysis indicated that the congregation currently has 100 parking spaces and a total income each year of $100,000 dollars. That means that the average income per year in relation to each parking space is $1,000 dollars. To add 100 new parking spaces may very well mean adding additional income of $100,000 per year over each of the coming five years. That constitutes a net new income of half a million dollars compared with the purchase price of $50,000 dollars for the property.

Frequently, a church committee thinks that the owner has placed too high a price on the adjacent property, and therefore, they conclude it does not make sense to purchase that land. Several years go by and the property is sold to another buyer, and the possibility of the church ever acquiring it becomes increasingly remote. This is not to suggest that the church should buy every piece of land for whatever price someone asks. Rather, it is simply to state that a responsible way to proceed is to calculate the cost of the new spaces in relation to the total net new income that can be projected over a reasonable period of time.

A Winning Combination

Thus, a winning combination is adequate parking, sufficient land, and aesthetically pleasing landscaping. This is not to suggest that rural churches should become "citified." Nor is it to suggest that churches in metropolitan areas should seek to look like their rural counterparts. Rather, it is simply to suggest that people form strong impressions of a congregation in relation to whether or not there is sufficient parking, land, and landscaping available and that it makes sense, therefore, to pay attention to these things.

The reader should not conclude that this is among the most important of the central characteristics of effective, successful churches. Indeed, this is the tenth characteristic and appropriately so. There may come a day when parking will not be as critical an issue as it is in the 1980s. That does not mean to suggest that a future oil shortage will force us to drive less; rather, it simply suggests that unless there is some major change in our cultural patterns, people will continue to depend upon automobiles as their principal mode of travel. Insofar as a church has a genuine interest in reaching additional people on behalf of Christ, that church will take seriously these factors of parking, land, and landscaping. A church that can be rated as 8, 9, or 10 on this central strength generally has a solid balance between its parking, land, and landscaping and its worship and church school attendance. Further, such a church tends to have additional parking for unchurched persons as they become increasingly interested in the life and mission of that congregation.

Rating Guide: Sufficient Parking

Item	Maximum Points	Your Church's Rating
1. Does the available off-street church parking (see Figure 10.1, #5) provide enough spaces for the number of people when the sanctuary is [select only one]:		
uncomfortably crowded	40	
comfortably filled	35	
comfortably empty	20	_____
uncomfortably empty	5	
or Does the church depend on on-street parking alone?	5	
2. Does the church own enough land for its present needs and future growth?	35	_____
3. Does the landscaping contribute to a first impression of warmth, welcome, and caring?	25	_____
Total:	100	_____

INSTRUCTIONS:

- Use the information in the chapter as a resource in evaluating your church's rating in each of the listed items.
- Enter the rating numbers in the blanks and then find the total.
- Divide the total of your assessment score by 10 to obtain your church's rating on a scale of 1 to 10.
- Enter that rating on the rating scale for Sufficient Parking in Figure C.1.

11. Adequate Space and Facilities

The Mistake of Underbuilding

Most churches underbuild rather than overbuild. For every large church that is uncomfortably empty, there are scores of churches that are uncomfortably crowded. Basically, too many churches have limited their growth potential because they have underbuilt their space and facilities.

To be sure, one can point to any number of downtown churches that are uncomfortably empty. The remaining congregation rattles around in the huge space and facilities, thinking that they made the mistake of overbuilding. In some instances, that conclusion is accurate. Even as that downtown church is uncomfortably empty, and even as many of its members have moved some considerable distance away, nevertheless the irony is that within average trip time of that congregation the population may have doubled or tripled in the last ten years.

More often than not, churches do make the mistake of underbuilding. They make the further mistake of designing inadequate space and facilities and then seeking to squeeze their programs and missional activities into them. The more constructive way to proceed is to design the long-range mission and programs of the congregation and only *then* to put in place adequate space and facilities to enable those programs and that mission to be effective.

An Analysis of the Congregation's Space and Facilities

Major Uses and Maximum Utilization

Four principal areas must be considered by a congregation as it seeks to analyze whether or not this central characteristic is well in place as an 8, 9, or 10. The first of these focuses on the major uses of the current space and facilities and the extent to which maximum utilization of these spaces is presently being achieved.

One way to assess this is to develop a floor plan of the facilities and then to mark on it the frequency of use of each of the various facilities on a week-to-week basis. In this fashion it will be possible to determine (1) the major uses of the space and facilities during an average week, (2) the principal areas of crowding, (3) any potential uses of space that are yet available, and (4) the extent to which maximum utilization of the space and facilities is taking place.

When a local congregation underbuilds its space and facilities, it is immediately prevented from developing maximum utilization of its space and facilities. The reason for this is quite simple. More often than not, the congregation that underbuilds does so by taking the original set of plans and reducing the square footage of each space in that set of plans until it matches the dollars available. Thus, a church school classroom that was originally planned to be sufficiently large that it could be used for a wide range of programs and activities is now reduced in size to such an extent that its uses are also severely limited. The extent to which a congregation builds space and facilities that are large and flexible in use determines the extent to which the congregation is likely to be able to develop a maximum utilization plan.

Balance

The second area of analysis of space and facilities is the matter of balance, that is, adequate space and facilities commensurate in size and capacity of use with one another. The key areas that should have balance are the sanctuary, the fellowship hall, the church school classrooms, the office area, and the parking. Frequently, I have discovered a church plan wherein the sanctuary is far too small in capacity in relation to the range of church school classrooms. Further, the fellowship hall is frequently too small to accommodate the number of people who are likely to participate in programs and activities there in relation to the number of people who participate each Sunday in worship.

Now, the ratio of balance will vary from one part of the country to another and from one congregation to another, depending largely on the focal points of that congregation's programs and activities. Certainly, several general relationships of balance can be suggested. It should be understood that these are intended as suggestions and will vary considerably from one local church to another.

1. If the sanctuary can accommodate approximately 100 people when it is comfortably filled, then it is important that the church school classes have a comfortably filled capacity of 125 to 150 people.
2. If the maximum comfortably filled capacity of the church school space is 150 then it would be important to have approximately 85 to 95 parking spaces.
3. Given the comfortably filled capacities of both the sanctuary and church school space, it would be important to have a fellowship hall that will accommodate from 125 to 175 people.

Now, this is not to suggest that every local church should have a sanctuary, church school space, and a fellowship hall. Indeed, many local congregations do not have all three of these facilities. The point is simply that it does not make sense to build any one of the three facilities unless there is some reasonable balance between the size of that facility and the other facilities that are in place or that are planned for construction at a later time. The key point is a sensible balance between space and facilities and the parking that the congregation makes available to its people and the community.

Condition and Improvements

The third area to analyze in assessing whether a given congregation has adequate space and facilities is the condition of those facilities and the improvements that might be necessary in order to put them in substantially good condition. The condition of the church's property communicates a strong message about how well that congregation thinks of itself. To put it another way, congregations who for a variety of reasons have developed low self-esteem tend to neglect their space and facilities. That is not to say that when you find space and facilities neglected you can immediately assume that the cause is low self-esteem; it may simply be that the financial resources of that congregation have been invested elsewhere in mission and program.

At the same time, the condition of the church's space and facilities does communicate a strong message to unchurched people in the community about how that church thinks of itself. The more adequate the condition and the more straightforwardly the congregation improves its space and facilities, the more likely that unchurched people are to think of that congregation as strong and solid.

This is not to suggest extravagant expenditures to achieve sound condition and improvements of quality. Rather, it is to suggest that people do judge a congregation on the appearance of its facilities. A rundown building that has been allowed to stand in disrepair for a number of years creates a certain kind of impression; a building that looks reasonably clean and well kept creates a different kind of impression and, furthermore, sets a standard for the homes and other kinds of buildings in that community.

Specific Considerations

The fourth part of an analysis of adequate space and facilities is a careful assessment of particular areas.

Sanctuary. The sanctuary is adequate when it is comfortably filled or comfortably empty. Please note that a sanctuary is not adequate if it is uncomfortably empty. Adequate does not always mean "big enough." It is also related to people's perceptions of comfort. The sanctuary that is uncomfortably crowded or uncomfortably empty is not adequate. A sanctuary can not only be too small; it can also be too big.

Church School. Basically church school classrooms should have a minimum size of approximately 400 square feet for every fifteen to twenty people. In a given church, if five church school rooms had this much space, five had more than this amount of space, and two did not have this much space, that would be considered adequate. If five church school rooms had this much space, two had more than this much space and five had less than this much space, that would be verging on inadequate.

This guideline suggests that church school classrooms of the future should be built to be flexible and highly usable spaces for a wide range of age groups. Given construction costs and energy factors, it is no longer feasible to build church school classrooms that are designed in narrow ways to be used by only one age group. A size of approximately 400 square feet is not a hard and fast rule, but it is an accurate guideline on which to base judgments as to the adequacy of church school space.

Fellowship Hall. The fellowship hall is adequate in relation to the capacity it has for the range of activities that take place there. Therefore, it is important to think of the fellowship hall in terms not only of the range of activities that take place there now, but of any future activities that you hope will be held there.

A related consideration has come forward with the emergence of multipurpose recreation facilities. Normally, it is not feasible for a congregation to have both a fellowship hall and a multipurpose recreation facility. The multipurpose recreation facility (sometimes referred to as a family life center) may also serve as the fellowship hall. The basic point is to list the range of activities that it makes sense to hold in that space and, from that, to ascertain its long-term adequacy or inadequacy.

Restrooms. Adequacy of restroom space must be judged primarily in relation to the morning church school and worship services. Though there are other times when restroom spaces are in use, the Sunday morning church school and worship services usually attract the largest groups of people. Therefore, simply determine the number of persons that your present restroom spaces can service in a fifteen- to twenty-minute period. That is, determine the adequacy of these spaces in terms of their maximum usage between church school and church. Then, match that factor with your average worship and church school attendance, and you will have some idea as to whether or not the restroom spaces are sufficiently large.

Nursery and Kindergarten. Two factors affect the adequacy of the nursery and kindergarten areas: (*a*) space and (*b*) design. With regard to space, most churches mistakenly think that since children are smaller than adults they need less space; they then pick the smallest room that can be found for the nursery, place some cribs very close together, and assume that this will be adequate. This assumption is erroneous.

Children frequently need *more* space than adults, whether they be in the nursery, toddler, or kindergarten age range or somewhat older. The key point about space is to analyze the extent to which these spaces provide for the range of activities for nursery, toddler, and kindergarten children.

Regarding design, it is important that the church's nursery and kindergarten be designed in relation to today's parents rather than the parents of the 1950s. The nursery and kindergarten need to communicate a sense of security and warmth to the parents of nursery, toddler, and kindergarten children. It is finally the parents who bring or who do not bring their children to these spaces. Regrettably, too many churches have nursery and kindergarten spaces that were designed by adults whose children were young in the 1950s but have since grown up. Textures, colors, lighting, and equipment should be obtained in consultation with parents who have small children in the 1980s. Some nurseries communicate that they are simply out of date, not because they're really out of date, but because they were designed with the textures and colors that were prevalent in the 1950s but which are no longer used by parents in the 1980s.

Storage. It's difficult to describe adequate storage. Mostly, congregations do not have it. In large part it depends on the individual church's storage needs. Therefore, I would simply encourage you to consider the range of storage space available and to take into account health and fire precautions in relation to these storage spaces. It might be worth considering renting a small unit in a miniwarehouse for storage of once-a-year items.

Arrangement. A final factor to consider is that of the arrangement of the space and facilities. The way the facilities are arranged can influence a vistor's perception of their adequacy. It is important that the arrangement makes them easy to locate. Further, it is important that the various hallways and corridors be sufficiently large and be arranged in a way that facilitates ease of movement. An arrangement like a jigsaw puzzle communicates a negative image even when the space and facilities themselves are quite adequate.

These basic guidelines will help you assess the adequacy of specific spaces within the congregation's total facilities. It may be helpful to invite two or three persons whose judgment you trust and respect to reflect with you on the adequacy of the church's space and facilities. It would be best to select people who are unfamiliar with the space and facilities so that you will have the chance of learning their first impressions. In that way, you will gain some understanding of the first impression of unchurched persons who visit your congregation.

Building and Growing

The First Unit

In developing future plans for adequate space and facilities, there are five areas of consideration that should be mentioned. For new congregations, it is important to note the following foundational principle: The first unit shapes all subsequent units. This principle has to do with more than simply whether or not there is a long-range master plan. Basically, what is at stake here is that the size and shape of the first unit determine the number of people that that congregation is likely to serve. The number of people that the congregation serves in its first unit determines in turn its capacity to build a second unit. More often than not, new congregations make the mistake of building the first unit too small. They then invest several years in trying to pay off that unit. By the time they have paid it off and are ready to build a second unit, the growth and development of that community have passed them by.

It would be better for most new congregations to spend a little longer period of time meeting in temporary facilities, such as the school auditorium, and then build a substantial first unit. In some instances the first unit may turn out to be the only unit that congregation builds. In that case, it is particularly important that it be reasonably adequate. In other instances, that first unit may be of sufficient size that it will attract an increasing number of people, so that the congregation becomes even stronger in its capacity to move on with its plans to build a second unit.

A related consideration for the first unit is that it is important that new congregations build large flexible spaces rather than specialized small spaces. A frequent mistake is for the new congregation to try and duplicate a large church plant in "mini" form. Regrettably, new congregations build too many church school facilities that are focused on specialized age ranges, but because of limitations of money, the size of the classrooms is not much larger than a walk-in closet or a small bedroom.

New congregations should build large enough so that they can continue to grow. Further, they should build with as small an investment of money up front as possible. Generally speaking, this means *not* building the sanctuary first. Overall, sanctuaries are more expensive spaces to build per cubic foot than are fellowship halls and church school classrooms.

When possible, new congregations should take advantage of a hillside by building a two-story facility that sets into the side of a modest hill.

Generally speaking, such a facility is less expensive to build. Moreover, it is possible to provide ground-level entry for handicapped persons on both levels. Such a facility is generally less expensive in terms of construction costs and utilities than a one-story campus-style building. To be sure, there are exceptions to this in various parts of the country, but new congregations should at least give this appropriate consideration.

Flexibility

Given the enormous rise in construction costs, loan payments and interest rates, and utility expenses, it is important that a congregation develop a range of flexible spaces that can be used by a variety of groups. It is no longer reasonable to build facilities that are used by one group for a few hours per week. The art of maximum utilization of space and facilities will increasingly be the design of highly flexible spaces.

This does not mean the groups should be moved around from one space to another year after year. Indeed, I have increasingly recommended that church school classes continue to meet from one year to the next in essentially the same space. In the children's division, the practice of promoting the children from one room to the next has been in vogue for a number of years. The practice came with the notion that very specialized rooms must be designed for given age ranges of children. To some extent, the thought has been that it is easier to move the children from one room to another than it is to move the various sizes of furniture that accommodate different sizes of children.

As churches build increasingly flexible spaces it becomes more important that church school classes and other groups have the sense of a room that is home. Flexibility does not mean shifting a group from one space to another. Rather, flexibility means that several groups share a given space over the course of an average week's usage. In some consultations, I have recommended that the churches design their space and facilities in such a way that each space be used approximately twenty or more hours per week.

It seems perfectly appropriate that a given church school class of kindergarten children continue to meet in the same space as they are promoted through elementary school together. Certainly, this would mean shifting the furniture. But the advantages of providing a group with a sense of roots, place, and belonging is an important consideration, given the highly mobile character of our culture. To be sure, this would mean that this group would develop some sense of "joint ownership" with the other groups who may use that flexible space at other times during the week. Any difficulties in this approach can be overcome by cooperation among the leaders of the various groups.

In the years to come, I foresee more difficulty arising from building highly specialized facilities for given age ranges than from helping groups learn how to live and share the same flexible space, however diverse those groups may be. The cost of construction, the cost of the loans and interest rates, and the cost of utilities mandate the development of flexible spaces in which several groups can feel at home.

Cost-Effectiveness

Obviously, there is direct correlation between the basic point of flexibility and the enormously powerful issue of cost-effectiveness. Finally, cost-effectiveness of space and facilities must be assessed in relation to two factors: (1) the maximum utilization of each space and facility in an average week and (2) the life expectancy of that specific space, given normal wear and tear. In the coming years, it will be imperative that congregations take cost-effectiveness seriously.

This does not mean that the appropriate thing for a congregation to do is to build inexpensive space and facilities. That is the poorest approach to cost-effectiveness. By the same token, it is important that congregations not build "gingerbread" facilities that have extraordinarily expensive ornamentation and decor. The facilities should be highly usable and be a strong symbol of mission. They should not be a monument to some architect, some pastor, or some group of lay leaders.

A detailed analysis of cost-effectiveness of any building project would include (1) the original construction costs, (2) the interest and principal payments on any loans, (3) the maximum usage in an average week, (4) the cost of utilities and normal repairs, (5) the cost of major preventive maintenance, (6) the projected life expectancy of the facility, (7) the number of persons who will be served over the course of years by this building project, and (8) the new income that this building project will eventually generate. These details will give a long-range planning committee the information it needs to assess the extent to which the proposed space and facilities will be genuinely cost-effective.

Preventive Maintenance

It is less expensive and more effective to develop a long-range preventive maintenance plan for a church's space and facilities than it is to repair them when emergencies occur. Indeed, it is important that a congregation put well in place such a preventive maintenance plan within five to seven years after the space and facilities have been built. Otherwise, the normal operating budget of the church will be continually under stress from major repairs that must be done unexpectedly and without sufficient reserve funds to take care of them.

This does not mean that a church should invest large sums of money in maintenance. A plan for preventive maintenance enables a church to provide thoughtfully and wisely for those items that should be cared for year by year rather than waiting for them to pile up, with the attendant possibility of exorbitant expense. For example, it is less expensive and more effective to systematically paint several rooms per year in a church school building than it is to wait five to seven years to paint all of the rooms at once. Obviously, the number will depend on the size of the building and the number of rooms it contains. But, generally speaking, it is less expensive to paint three rooms a year over the course of four years than it is to paint all twelve rooms at the higher rate likely to be charged four years from now. Certainly, some will suggest that it is easier to get it done en masse because a paint contractor will do the big job for less. That may be the case in some instances.

But over the long haul, a preventive maintenance plan does something equally as important as saving money. The regular, systematic renewal and restoration of spaces, based on a preventive maintenance plan, also enables the congregation to experience something "new" each year. The older a facility is, the more important it is to do this. Some congregations desire to have something new, and build additional space and facilities— not because they are really necessary in the long term, but because they want something new. Across the country, one can see church school annexes that were built mainly to satisfy this desire. The simpler, easier, and less expensive way to do this is to have a preventive maintenance plan that delivers to the congregation something new on a regular basis and enables them to experience their space and facilities with a kind of freshness and vitality that it is important to feel.

Build to Grow

In the unchurched culture of the coming years, it is important to build in order to grow. We used to assume that one must grow and then build. Generally, the way that assumption worked out was that a congregation would grow to an overcrowded condition; then it would build much needed space and facilities in order to alleviate the overcrowding already present in the congregation. But, seldom did that congregation build enough to accommodate the range of unchurched persons with which it could be in mission, were it desirous of doing so. More often than not, a congregation would move into its additional space and facilities and find that it was immediately overcrowded once again. In the heyday of the church boom, one built space and facilities to alleviate overcrowded conditions. Local congregations still have too much of the 1950s understanding of space and facilities.

It is important for congregations to understand that they can build to grow. That is, they do not have to wait until they have grown in order to build; rather, they can build adequate space and facilities—wisely located—and put in place a strong missional outreach. Those congregations will be likely to grow.

Now, a congregation that shares strong missional outreach, pastoral and lay visitation, corporate and dynamic worship, and significant relational groups can overcome the disadvantage of being crowded into inadequate space and facilities. It can survive for a number of years because it is providing the relational strengths in such compelling fashion that people will put up with being overcrowded.

By the same token, a congregation that provides mission, visitation, worship, and groups that are strong enough to be rated 8, 9, or 10 and *also* provides adequate space and facilities is a congregation that can build those facilities in order to grow rather than waiting for the growth and then trying to build. It is wise investment in space and facilities, combined with strong relational strengths, that enables a church to develop an extraordinary outreach in a community. The basic point is that a congregation should think through whether or not the time is right to build in order to grow and then have the confidence to do so, even as it reinforces the relational strengths that will be important in advancing its growth.

A House and a Home

Space and facilities are finally comparable to the house in which a family lives. A house does not make a home; people do. Some pastors and key leaders assume that when they have fine, new facilities they will therefore have a strong corporate community in the life of the congregation. That is not the case. Indeed, new space and facilities provide only a momentary source of satisfaction. There is a fleeting time in which the congregation takes pride in its accomplishment.

But the enduring sources of satisfaction present within any congregation will come from the strength of the relational characteristics of an effective, successful church. One reason so many pastors move so soon after they have completed a building program is that they do not understand this basic principle.

The quality of mission and the quality of life together, shared with one another and with the community at large, determine the extent to which the space and facilities are "home" or simply a house. People do look for roots, place, and belonging—and they do associate roots, place, and belonging with given spaces in their own lives. Insofar as people discover community within a congregation, to that extent they will sense that this space and these facilities are home for them.

Rating Guide: Adequate Space and Facilities

Item	Maximum Points	Your Church's Rating
1. Do the major uses contribute to mission, program, and the utilization of the facilities?	35	_____
2. Are the spaces in balance with one another?	35	_____
3. Are the facilities maintained in good condition, and improvements planned?	30	_____
Total:	100	_____

INSTRUCTIONS:

- Use the information in the chapter as a resource in evaluating your church's rating in each of the listed items.
- Enter the rating numbers in the blanks and then find the total.
- Divide the total of your assessment score by 10 to obtain your church's rating on a scale of 1 to 10.
- Enter that rating on the rating scale for Adequate Space and Facilities in Figure C.1.

12. Solid Financial Resources

Stewardship and Investment

Solid financial resources is the twelfth characteristic of effective, successful congregations. It is decisive that a thoughtful theology of stewardship undergird the development of solid financial resources in every local church. "Saving money" does not constitute an adequate stewardship theology. Indeed, the notion that the purpose of stewardship is to help a congregation to conserve its funds is, in fact, counter to the biblical witness.

A responsible theology of stewardship encourages local congregations to invest money in such a way as to (1) increase missional services in the community, (2) maximize the effectiveness of the local church, and (3) add to the number of households that contribute financially to the life and mission of the congregation. It is not the task of the church to save money. Nor is it the task of the church to spend money. Rather, it is vitally important that the church invest its funds wisely so that mission, effectiveness, and increased giving are the substantive results of its sound "investments."

Some of these investments will be in mission, some in people, some in programs, and some in sound financial development plans. Local congregations should avoid foolish spending, but they should also avoid foolish saving. In these times, it is extraordinarily important that congregations think through seriously the ways in which the expenditure of their funds constitutes solid investment on behalf of the life and mission of the church.

Income and Resources

Current Income

Five factors should be considered in any analysis of whether or not a given local church has solid financial resources. The first is current income. Most congregations have more current income than they think they do. Regrettably, too many congregations think of current income only in relation to their operating budget for the present year. As a matter of fact, local churches receive considerably more contributions in a given year than are designated solely for the operating budget. A thoughtful analysis of a congregation's financial situation would take

Figure 12.1 Total Current Income Analysis

Indicate the per capita giving in relation to average worship attendance, and church membership for the past seven years. For this analysis use the total income of the church (regular giving, special gifts, endowment income, service fees, etc.). For example, if the total income in first year shown was $100,000 and average worship attendance was 200, then per capita giving in relation to average worship attendance would be $500. If membership was 500, then per capita giving in relation to membership would be $200.

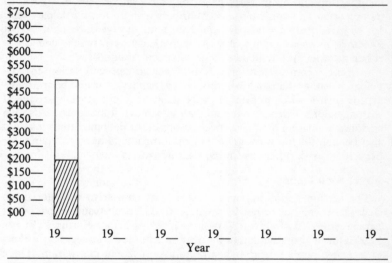

□—Average Worship Attendance

▨—Membership

seriously the total contributions that a church receives in a given year. That is a better indicator of the strength and vitality of the congregation's giving.

Further, a thoughtful analysis would relate the total income of the church to average worship attendance, as well as to church membership. The chart above shows how this can be graphically illustrated. The arithmetic involved looks like this:

$$\frac{\text{Total Income}}{\text{Average Worship Attendance}} = \text{per capita income from people attending worship.}$$

$$\frac{\text{Total Income}}{\text{Church Membership}} = \text{per capita income from church members.}$$

A different figure could likewise be determined by dividing total income by the number of households, or giving units, represented in the average worship attendance.

Over time, these graphs usually show that income goes up in relation to increased participation, not increased membership. Thus, a congregation that wishes to increase its total income should work more strongly on increasing worship and church school attendance than on increasing membership. There is very little correlation between an increase in membership and an increase in giving; the key correlation is between participation and contributions. Members who do not participate tend not to give. People who participate do tend to give. The church that increases its membership may not experience very much increase in either its worship attendance or its total contributions.

Current income, therefore, is best considered in relation to participation rather than membership. Given that fact, it would be appropriate for each local church to compare its average giving per participant with appropriate denominational data to achieve some sense of its own standing in relation to other congregations in the denomination. It would also be helpful for a congregation to compare its average giving per participant with others in similar denominations.

Net New Income

The second factor important for a local church to consider in an analysis of whether or not its financial resources are solid is that of net new income. The following Mission-Growth-Finance Formula (Figure 12.2) is one way of calculating the net new income a congregation is likely to receive directly related to a strong mission visitation program. There are other ways to compute net new income as well. It is obvious that projected increases in worship attendance can be translated directly to net new income for instance. However, for our present purposes, the Mission-Growth-Finance formula will be useful in projecting one source of net new income.

The Mission-Growth-Finance formula is not intended to focus on net new income for its own sake. Rather, the mission visitation program should be seen as an important program in its own right. Indeed, it is decisive that congregations be in mission with households whether they ever become participants in the life and mission of that congregation or not. Frankly, I am perfectly willing to show a local church the net new income and the net new members so that they can also see the mission. To use the example cited below, it may be helpful for a local church to know that its five-year commitment to such a mission visitation is likely to yield $283,500 in additional funds. Further, it may be helpful for that congregation to know that such a program will enable it to reach 192

Figure 12.2   Mission-Growth-Finance Formula

1. From the results of the mission visitation program (Figure 2.2), determine the total number of persons from this 20–33% who will become involved in the life and mission of your local church.

   On an average, these 38–63 families from the example in Figure 2.2 will include two or three persons per family. This will likely result in 76–114 persons (20%) to 126–189 persons (33%) becoming involved in your local church. (Multiply step 4 in Figure 2.2 by 2 or 3.) Of these, approximately 40% will become members and 60%, constituents.

   Total number of persons who will
   become involved in your church. _____

2. Calculate the number of "giving units" that will emerge in relation to the percentage of families and persons who become active in the local church. A 30% shrinkage factor is normal. (Take 30% of step 4 from Figure 2.2.) That would mean that 27 "giving units" would emerge from among the 38 families, based on reaching 20% of the missional 192 families; 44, if 33% are reached.

   Total number of giving units that will emerge. _____

3. Estimate the total net new income per year that will result from these "giving units."

   Multiply the number of giving units by the average annual giving per unit currently in church. For example, 27 giving units at $700 per year yields $18,900 per year of net new income.

   *Total net new income per year. $*_____

4. Decide the long-term commitment that this mission visitation program will have in the local church.

   Multiply the annual net new income on a geometrical basis in relation to the number of years of commitment. For example, a church that makes a five-year commitment to the above program will receive $283,500 as the total new income for that period.

   In this example, it is projected that 27 new giving units per year will become participants in a particular local church during the coming five years. Over the course of this five-year period, the first year's 27 new giving units will contribute each of the five years. The second year's 27 new giving units will contribute four of the five years, and so on. This geometrical factor results in a total of 15 giving-year periods over the course of the five years. Thus the average contribution per year in the example of $18,900 is multiplied by a factor of 15 to yield the total net new income for the five-year period.

   This church's long-term commitment to this mission visitation program will be for_____years.

   *Total net new income for this period $*_____

households who are likely to become members and participants. But it is much more important for the congregation to know that such a mission visitation program will enable them to be in mission with 770 households over a five-year period.

The importance of that mission with these 770 households is to share with them effective help with their own human hurts and hopes, whether they ever become members or participants in the congregation or not. Any church that has been reasonably effective with 770 households in its community will be, in fact, a legend on the community grapevine. These 770 households will be a major network of referral that will enable that congregation to advance its effective help in the community even more substantially in the years to come.

To be sure, for the purpose of evaluating solid financial resources it is important to consider net new income. At the same time, it is important for the local congregation to see the strength of its mission in the community as having major priority. To some extent, this will enable the local church to be in mission for the sake of mission and to experience any income that is net new income as a by-product of that mission. The income is not the end in itself—the mission is the objective toward which the local church heads. The increase in giving simply comes, if it does, as a useful by-product.

Endowment and Assets

The third factor to consider in an analysis of financial resources is the endowment and assets of the local church. Endowment relates to the principal that the church has set aside, using the interest to endow specific mission, program, or property items. This is not to suggest that a church does not have solid financial resources if it lacks an endowment fund; rather it is to suggest that endowment funds constitute one large source of assets for a congregation.

Assets are also property, space and facilities, stocks, bonds, and other liquid and capital assets a congregation has gathered over the years. No church can adequately assess its financial resources without doing a careful analysis of all of the endowment funds it may have and all of the assets that constitute the results of the financial resources that the congregation has put in place in prior years.

Indebtedness

The fourth factor to consider is indebtedness. Analysis of indebtedness should look at more than simply the amount of money a church owes in debts and obligations. Rather, it should focus on the amount of the debt, the interest rate, and the schedule of payments. In these times, it is not necessarily the most advisable course of action to pay off a particular debt as quickly as possible. Indeed, a church that has a loan at an interest rate that is less than 10 percent may be wiser not to pay off that debt too quickly.

The basic point is that there should be some appropriate balance between current income, net new income, endowment and asset funds, and indebtedness.

It may be appropriate that a church have continuing indebtedness if it has invested those funds wisely in advancing the future mission and outreach of the congregation. In that sense, the church has made a wise investment in relation to the indebtedness it has incurred. At the same time, that indebtedness must be balanced in relation to the factors mentioned above and the potential financial resources.

Potential Financial Resources

It is possible for a local congregation to do an analysis of the occupational groups that are present in its life and mission. Then, that congregation may obtain data from the local census bureau or county planning agency about the average income in that region for the occupational categories that it has discovered are present in the congregation. With this data, the church can make a thoughtful assessment of the potential financial resources it has available.

Many congregations underestimate the potential financial resources present in the church and in the community. It is with some wisdom that I say "in the church and in the community." It is well for a local church to know that it can count on a range of financial resources from the community insofar as that local church designs and advances a worthwhile project to attract those community contributions.

Although estimating potential financial resources is a matter of judgment, the use of the occupational categories and related income averages will make it possible to develop a more responsible estimate of the potential financial resources than would be possible simply by estimating in generalities what those resources might be. Given these five factors, it is possible for a long-range planning committee to assess the adequacy of that congregation's financial resources.

Development of Resources

Money Follows Mission

It is important to note that money follows mission, not the reverse. To be sure, on some occasions it may be the case that mission follows money. Indeed, there are persons who have made the false assumption that mission is limited by money; only in rare instances is that accurate.

More often than not, the reason a congregation does not have enough money is that it has not effectively delivered substantive mission in that community. It has become preoccupied with maintenance and forgotten mission. Whenever a local church does that, it can count on the giving diminishing. People give to mission more than they give to maintenance.

Now, I am aware of the myth that people would rather build buildings than give to mission causes. Frankly, the reason they give for those buildings is that the buildings are sufficiently specific and concrete that they can see objectively how their giving is being used. Those congregations that have been as specific and concrete in the development of their mission objectives tend to have much less difficulty in raising funds to achieve those missional objectives.

The congregation that sends out the following message can expect to receive only a small return: "We've gotten a little bit behind on our income. We've tried to do about the best we can. Would you please give a little more to help us catch up?"

Those churches that are most effective in raising funds tend to share the following message: "Our church is helping many people. We are delivering effective help. Your funds are being invested wisely and well. Thanks for your giving." The church that approaches the matter in this fashion tends to raise more funds. In short, the church that has a small mission tends to raise a small amount of money. The church that has a substantial mission tends to raise a substantial amount of money.

People Give to People

People give to people. Next, people give to purposes and causes. Next, people give to programs. Finally, people give to paper—in response to brochures and letters. When funds are successfully raised, the primary reason is that people give to people. Who asks for the money is as important as the purpose for the money or the number of pieces of paper that have been sent to households about it. The most effective forms of fund raising are relational, not functional.

Earlier, I said that people live in three neighborhoods: a relational neighborhood, a sociological neighborhood, and a geographical neighborhood. The strongest and most effective neighborhood is the relational neighborhood. To the extent that a fund-raising strategy builds on the relational neighborhood that is already in place, that church will raise substantial funds. Local churches that depend on the sociological and the geographical neighborhoods as the primary arenas in which they raise funds will be less successful.

For example, the widely used "pony express" strategy is based on the principle of a person's carrying the saddle bags from his or her house to a nearby house. It would be far better to organize the pony express routes around the relational neighborhood than the geographical neighborhood. To be sure, that might mean that people would carry the saddle bags two miles away rather than two blocks away. At the same time, it is likely to be an extraordinarily more effective visit insofar as the person has been asked to carry the saddle bags to a friend, acquaintance, or a family member rather than someone who simply lives down the block.

People give to people in whom they sense mutual trust, respect, and integrity. People's assessment of how worthwhile the cause is to which they are being asked to contribute has a direct relationship to the sense of trust, respect, and integrity they have for the person asking them to give. It is, therefore, extraordinarily important that the fund-raising strategy not build on gimmicks or cleverly worded letters. Rather, fund raising should build on the relationships of respect, trust, and integrity that are already solidly in place in the congregation.

Actual-Purchasing-Power Budgeting

Most congregations do straight-line budgeting. That is, as they look toward the budget for the coming year they list the specific line item, the amount designated for the previous year, the amount designated for the coming year, and the change—plus or minus. This straight-line budgeting approach does not give a congregation an accurate picture of the actual purchasing power of the budget it is preparing for the coming year.

A better way to achieve an accurate analysis is to use an actual-purchasing-power budget. For each specific line item there is the current year amount, there is an adjusted amount, there is the amount for the coming year, and there is the change—plus or minus. The adjusted current year amount reflects the amount needed for the purchasing power to achieve the same results in the coming year as are being achieved in the current year.

Both approaches are shown in Figure 12.3. The advantages of the actual-purchasing-power budget approach are apparent. It would take $440 in the coming year to purchase the same amount of church school supplies that is being purchased in the present year for $400, based on 10 percent inflation. (It is perfectly appropriate to use different figures for inflation as it affects different budget items.) Note that, considering the inflation factor, we have not increased the church school supplies budget by $100, but by $60. The value of an actual-purchasing-power budget approach is that it clearly sets forth the impact of inflation on the development of a budget.

Long-Range Planning

In coming years it will be increasingly important for local churches to develop a long-range budget plan, one that looks forward four years rather than just one; it is not easy to do effective financial management on an annual basis alone. To develop a budget for four years ahead, a

Figure 12.3 Budget Analysis Chart

Item	Current Year Amount	Adjusted Current Year Amount	Coming Year Amount	Plus/Minus Amount
Straight-Line Budgeting				
Church School Supplies	$400	—	$500	$100
Actual-Purchasing-Power Budgeting				
Church School Supplies	$400	$440	$500	$ 60

local church will need to develop strategic priorities for the major investments it plans to make during each of the coming four years.

Such a long-range plan does not mean developing specific line-item budget amounts for each of the four years. Rather, it means to have in mind a total budget goal for each of the coming four years. As a further breakdown, it may be possible to have in place amounts for at least the major budget divisions for the coming three years, and it is also appropriate to work out budgets for the primary department areas for the coming two years. It is necessary only to have a specific budget figure for each line-item for the coming year.

This approach enables a local church to develop a fund-raising strategy over the long term, which in turn makes it possible to develop fundraising strategies that build on each other from one year to the next. It is regrettable that too many churches think through the motivational and strategic approaches to fund raising only one year at a time. They never develop a sense of momentum toward increased contributions because they do not have the benefit of building from one year to the next. A four-year budget plan enables a congregation to have a four-year fundraising strategy as well.

One of the emerging, important features of a congregation's solid financial resources is effective long-range financial planning. Though this is a comparatively new art in local churches, it will become increasingly vital in the years ahead. And those churches that know where they are headed in terms of major missional objectives for the coming four years will be in the best position to develop an effective long-range financial plan.

Money and People

Having solid financial resources is the twelfth characteristic, not the first characteristic, of effective, successful churches. Again, the relational factors are more important than the functional factors. The people factors are more important than the money factors. This is not to say that money is unimportant; rather, it is to affirm that it is the twelfth most important factor in developing effective, successful congregations. It is important that solid financial resources have a rightful and appropriate place as one of the twelve central characteristics. At the same time, it must be stated forcefully that people are more important than money in the life and mission of the church. Wherever people are effectively helped, there is the strong likelihood that giving will follow. Wherever the preoccupation is income, there is the strong likelihood that people will not be helped and that people will not come to join that local congregation in its life and mission in the community.

Rating Guide: Solid Financial Resources

Item	Maximum Points	Your Church's Rating
1. Does the per capita income, based on average worship attendance, represent a reasonable level compared with denominational data?	25	_____
2. Based on the current mission efforts, can your church expect to benefit from an increase in giving (net new income—see formula, Figure 12.2)?	20	_____
3. Has the church established interest-bearing investments of its financial resources, as well as the property and space and facilities used in its mission?	15	_____
4. Is the financial indebtedness being managed advantageously in balance with the church's mission and outreach?	15	_____
5. Has the church taken seriously the potential financial resources available to it?	25	_____
Total:	100	_____

INSTRUCTIONS:

- Use the information in the chapter as a resource in evaluating your church's rating in each of the listed items.
- Enter the rating numbers in the blanks and then find the total.
- Divide the total of your assessment score by 10 to obtain your church's rating on a scale of 1 to 10.
- Enter that rating on the rating scale for Solid Financial Resources in Figure C.1.

Conclusion: Principles and Priorities in Strategic Long-Range Planning

Final Decisions

Given the material that has been shared in foregoing chapters, you should now be in a better position to develop final decisions that will advance the life and mission of your own congregation. The first step in strategic long-range planning has been to develop a realistic assessment of the congregation's present standing and stature in comparison with other congregations. The second step has been to decide the primary direction for that church's future. The third step has been to do a thoughtful study of that congregation's strengths in relation to the central characteristics of effective, successful churches. The fourth step is to make those final decisions that form the strategic long-range plan for that church.

Having studied each of the twelve central characteristics, it is now possible for you and/or the long-range planning committee to make reasonable judgments as to the strength and adequacy of the congregation in each of the twelve characteristics. Figure C.1 is provided to help accomplish this purpose.

Note that, first, each of the twelve characteristics should be ranked alone. No attempt should be made to rank "the top ten" characteristics. Rather, the function of the chart is to enable you and the long-range planning committee to assess each characteristic independently—where the church stands only in terms of that specific central characteristic.

Second, watch out for the naivete and platitudinal generosity of some long-range planning committees. The purpose of the summary chart is to accurately and realistically assess the degree of strength of each characteristic. The purpose of the chart is not for a long-range planning committee to "pat itself on the back" about how well in place all twelve of the characteristics are. Nor is the purpose of the chart for a long-range planning committee to confirm "how poorly our church is doing and what a terribly precarious state it is in." Neither of these perspectives is useful. Rather, the purpose of the summary chart is to diagram a thoughtful analysis that accurately and realistically portrays a specific congregation's present state.

Figure C.1 Summary Analysis of the Central Characteristics of Successful Churches

Relational Characteristics	_Functional Characteristics_

1. Specific, Concrete Missional Objectives
   1 2 3 4 5 6 7 8 9 10
	7. Several Competent Programs and Activities
	   1 2 3 4 5 6 7 8 9 10

2. Pastoral/Lay Visitation in Community
   1 2 3 4 5 6 7 8 9 10
	8. Open Accessibility
	   1 2 3 4 5 6 7 8 9 10

3. Corporate, Dynamic Worship
   1 2 3 4 5 6 7 8 9 10
	9. High Visibility
	   1 2 3 4 5 6 7 8 9 10

4. Significant Relational Groups
   1 2 3 4 5 6 7 8 9 10
	10. Adequate Parking
	   1 2 3 4 5 6 7 8 9 10

5. Strong Leadership Resources
   1 2 3 4 5 6 7 8 9 10
	11. Adequate Space and Facilities
	   1 2 3 4 5 6 7 8 9 10

6. Solid, Participatory Decision Making
   1 2 3 4 5 6 7 8 9 10
	12. Solid Financial Resources
	   1 2 3 4 5 6 7 8 9 10

This chart is to be used as a summary of the long-range planning committee's detailed study of the local church's present strengths. Using the Rating Guide at the end of the appropriate chapter, circle the number that most accurately and realistically reflects your church's strength in each of the above characteristics. Remember that the higher the number, the greater the degree of strength.

You and the long-range planning committee will want to use the rating guides at the end of each chapter to assist in this ranking before you circle the appropriate number under each characteristic to describe your church's present status on a scale of 1 to 10.

Here are four additional ways of using the summary chart. First, underline each characteristic that the church has well in place as 8, 9, or 10. Underlining will highlight those characteristics that are currently contributing to the effectiveness and success of that congregation. Second, out of those, "double underline"—that is, add a second line to—those strengths you think should be expanded during the coming five to seven years.

Third, circle those characteristics that are not now well in place, but that—at least in tentative ways—should be considered as future foundational strengths and could be added during the coming five to seven years. Fourth, put a tentative year in the margin indicating during which of the coming years it would make good sense to bring "on line" that specific expanded or added foundational strength.

By completing these four procedural steps, it will be possible to have a tentative vision of those strategic priorities that will advance the life and mission of the congregation.

Principles for Developing the Plan

Confidence and Competence

Develop a strategic long-range plan that builds confidence and competence in the early stages of the plan. This is the first of four principles that contribute strategically to the decisions about which strengths to expand and which strengths to add in the coming decisive years. As confidence and competence are built, it will become increasingly possible for a congregation to put in place a growing range of accomplishments and achievements in mission. It is sometimes useful to develop a long-range plan that delivers an immediate win in the early stages of the plan. That immediate win should be a reasonably visible achievement. This will be especially helpful to congregations that suffer from extraordinarily low self-esteem.

Now, it is important to distinguish this immediate win from a "quick-closure" venture. More often than not, quick closures focus on those priorities that are urgent but not important. An immediate win would focus instead on a strategic priority that is both important and urgent. It is the kind of strategic priority that can be reasonably accomplished within a modest span of time, so that the satisfaction level of the congregation is advanced. To be sure, there is a fine line between an immediate win and a quick closure venture; the key distinction is that the immediate win focuses on a priority that is *both* important and urgent. To boost the confidence and competence of the congregation as it moves on to tackle increasingly tough priorities is a sound first step.

Expand First

The second principle in developing a strategic long-range plan is to expand first those strengths that are easiest to expand. Obviously, this principle is related to the first principle. At the same time, it carries the matter forward with an additional insight. It is easier to expand a current foundational strength than it is to add a new one. Frequently, it takes one to three years to add a new foundational strength. More often than not, it is possible to expand a present strength considerably in six to eighteen months.

The important point to note is that it makes good sense to focus on expanding those present strengths that will be easiest to expand as we build the mission of a particular congregation. Another way of saying it is walk before you run. It is easier for a congregation to do better what it is already doing well than it is for the same conregation to do well what it is not doing well—at all. Therefore, the long-range planning committee should look with some discernment at which of those central strengths that presently rated 8, 9, or 10 can be naturally and easily expanded in the coming five to seven years.

Now, it is important to note that not all of the current strengths need to be expanded. Indeed, the committee that adopted a strategic plan that advocated expanding all of the current foundational strengths would have selected too many strategic priorities.

For example, a given congregation may rank very well in corporate, dynamic worship, significant relational groups, open accessibility, high visibility, sufficient parking, and adequate space and facilities. It would not make good sense for their long-range planning committee to develop a strategic plan advocating that all six of those current foundational strengths be expanded during the coming five to seven years. That would be working harder, not smarter. It might, however, make good sense for that committee to recommend that their strengths in worship and groups be considerably expanded at appropriate time intervals during the coming five to seven years. Indeed, they might suggest expanding a third current strength—namely, sufficient parking.

The point is that it is neither appropriate nor wise for a long-range planning committee simply to say that it is going to expand all of its current strengths during the coming five to seven years. It is the better part of wisdom to select two out of six current strengths and to design a strategic plan that will substantially expand those specific two strengths.

A Natural Rhythm

The third principle in formulating the strategic long-range plan is to develop a natural rhythm of expanding and adding foundational strengths. As you study the relationship of the twelve characteristics to one another, a natural rhythm of expanding and adding some of these twelve characteristics will become increasingly clear. It would not be the better part of wisdom for a committee to recommend adding new foundational strengths in three successive years. By the same token, it would not make good sense to have several years in which the only thing the congregation is doing is expanding its present strengths.

There is an appropriate, natural rhythm that is distinctively valuable for each congregation. It may well be that a long-range planning committee with some wisdom would suggest that in the first year a specific strength be expanded, and in the second year another strength added, in the third year two strengths expanded, in the fourth another strength added, and in the fifth year another strength expanded.

The basic point is not to overload a series of years back to back. It is easier to expand a current strength than it is to add a new one. Therefore, it makes good sense to interchange these from year to year—or, at least, over a two- to three-year period.

A common mistake is seeking to do too much too soon. It is important to build confidence and competence in the early stages of the long-range plan. It is equally important that the early stages not constitute an overload of too many and too ambitious a set of priorities. There is no point in increasing the low self-esteem and lack of confidence that many congregations have about themselves. A natural rhythm of expanding and adding provides opportunity for resting and gathering momentum to put in place new additions.

Complementary Priorities

The fourth principle in the strategic long-range plan is to develop complementary priorities that reinforce one another. Long-range planning committees frequently try to put well in place all twelve of the central characteristics of effective, successful churches. Even congregations that have as many as seven of the twelve characteristics well in place think that it is possible to expand some of the seven current strengths and to add five new foundational strengths in the course of a five to seven year plan. Such a venture is doomed to failure. The mistake is for long-range planning committees to try to expand current foundational strengths and add new ones that have no complementary relationship to each other.

The best long-range plans select a few strengths to expand, and even fewer to add, that constitute a complementary match. Thus, those strengths being expanded and those being added create a high degree of positive mutual reinforcement as the years of the strategic plan advance.

Now, it is not possible to describe out of the context of a given local church which of the twelve strengths will complement one another. In some local churches, expanding significant relational groups and adding strong leadership resources will constitute a complementary match. In other congregations, expanding the current strength of corporate, dynamic worship and adding, as a new strength, pastoral and lay visitation may constitute a match.

However, which strategic priorities will be complementary cannot be predicted from one congregation to another. Rather, it is vitally important that a long-range planning committee consider seriously the integrity and particularity of its own congregation so that it decides *for itself* those strengths that will complement one another. Local congregations are sufficiently distinctive so that this match must be considered case by case.

Priorities in Long-Range Planning

The promise of priorities is to give power to planning. In long-range planning, it is decisive to set forth strategic priorities that focus and energize the human and financial resources of the group toward significant accomplishments. Setting strategic priorities has implications—four illustrations of the function and power of priorities in an organization are set out in the following sections.

Priorities as Priorities

Priorities *are* priorities. Priorities are done first; they inform and shape the rest of our work. This is especially true of strategic priorities. Priorities make it possible for leaders to work smarter, not harder. Whenever leaders view priorities as "more work," they are not taking their function seriously. Strategic priorities are not simply "added on" to everything else the leaders of a local church are already doing. Rather, they give shape and direction to those things that continue to be done and those things the leaders cease doing. Strategic priorities have decisive consequences for what leaders do.

Further, strategic priorities inform and shape the work of everyone in the local church. It is not the case that a few people work directly toward the achievement of strategic priorities while the rest of the people continue "doing their own thing." It is of major importance that the leaders and workers as a team share corporately, creatively, and courageously in the achievement of the church's strategic priorities. That means that every person on the team contributes directly to the achievement of the strategic priorities.

Leaders and Workers

Whenever a church develops specific strategic priorities, it is imperative that adequate leaders and workers be solidly in place so that the priorities can be usefully and manageably achieved. Most churches are "top heavy" with priorities; that is, they have an abundance of priorities but a scarcity of leaders and workers. They have too many priorities. Such churches have set themselves up to fail. Generally speaking, matching the range of priorities with the range of leaders and workers is the best balance; that is, develop strategic priorities only commensurate with the leaders and workers available to accomplish them.

Program Reduction

Programs serve people. People are not to be slaves to programs. Most churches are overprogrammed. In our country, the myth has been perpetuated that an effective organization is one that has lots of programs; but that is not correct. An effective organization is one that helps people in competent, creative ways. Programs are only one way of helping people; indeed, it is more precise to say that *some* programs help people. Some programs are more harmful than they are helpful.

The function of strategic priorities is to provide "a razor's edge" to determine which programs make sense to continue, which programs need to be modified, and which programs should be cut out entirely.

There is no merit in the kingdom of God for the number of programs a local church has; there *is* some merit in the kingdom of God for the number of people who are genuinely helped with their lives. People help people. Programs do not help people. On occasion, some programs may facilitate people helping people, but whenever programs become ends in themselves, they are no longer effective in enabling people to help people.

Many churches could reduce the number of their programs by 25 percent without in any way lessening the range or number of people who are being helped. Indeed, such a reduction might free leaders and workers to have more time to help people rather than participate in programs. As a matter of fact, the function of strategic priorities is to provide guidance to a church so that it can more responsibly and thoughtfully know where such program reductions can best take place.

Streamlined Organization and Committee Work

In churches we sometimes find too many committees and too many people on committees to do effective work. Organizational structures tend to be designed to function effectively in medium-sized organizations. Large organizations assume that by adding people to committees and adding more committees they can staff a medium-sized organizational structure. Clearly, neither is useful. Medium-sized organization structures work best in medium-sized organizations.

It is appropriate and important that a local church design an organizational structure that will work effectively in that size of organization. Generally speaking, the larger the organization, the more important it is to have a streamlined organizational structure. Large churches must justify their existence by the effectiveness, directness, and quickness with which they respond to human hurts and hopes. The more tiresome and cumbersome the decision-making process in the church, the more that church loses its justification for existing as an organization. In some churches, the truism has been: The larger we become, the more time we spend in committees and the less time we spend effectively helping people. It is substantially important, therefore, that a church have only as many committees as are absolutely necessary. It is imperative that a committee have only as many people on it as is necessary to achieve wise, creative decisions and to implement and accomplish central priorities related to that committee's authority and responsibilities.

The strategic priorities make it possible for an organization to decide which committees it ought to have to achieve them. Form follows function. Organizational structure should follow key objectives, not the other way around. Just as strategic priorities make it possible to do straightforward programming, so also those same strategic priorities make it possible for an organization to have a streamlined approach to its committees and structure. The rule of thumb is a lean organizational structure that enables the organization to deliver results in relation to its strategic priorities.

Strategic Long-Range Planning: Conclusion

Long-Range Planning as an Art

Strategic long-range planning is more an art than it is a science. To be sure, I thoughtfully consider a range of statistics and data that are useful in discerning the extent to which a congregation has the twelve central characteristics well in place. Further, I have developed and used widely certain formulas that have proven to be extraordinarily helpful in predicting the present and future strength capabilities in certain of the central characteristics. Moreover, I have found the rating sheets, which are included at the end of each of the chapters related to the central characteristics, helpful indicators of whether or not that characteristic is well in place in a given congregation. At the same time, I am wise enough to know that strategic long-range planning is primarily an art, not a science. The twelve central characteristics, the specific formulas that have been developed, and the detailed rating sheets are suggestive of the strength and vitality of the congregation, and they provide modest indicators toward the development of a strategic long-range plan. The leaders of a congregation—on occasion with the assistance of a competent consultant—must finally trust their wisdom, judgment, and vision about those strengths that it makes sense to expand, those strengths it makes sense to add, and the time sequence of those strategic priorities.

The art of strategic long-range planning is to create a set of strategic priorities that enables us to behave responsibly and courageously in the present, advance toward a future of more substantive mission in the community, and keep open our alternatives for the future. The purpose of strategic long-range planning is not to box in the future. The purpose of strategic long-range planning is not to put in place such an exact plan that there is no freedom or flexibility in the years to come. Rather, the art of strategic long-range planning is to develop the natural sequence of steps in such a fashion that—as best we can—the future is kept open. That is, as new possibilities and alternatives emerge it will be possible to shape the direction of the church's strategic priorities to meet the new calling of God to be in mission in even newer and stronger ways.

The flexibility and freedom of strategic long-range planning is gained from the wisdom, judgment, and vision of leaders of the congregation. I would in no way advocate a flexibility or freedom that falls victim to the whims, fads, and foolishness that sweep through the church from year to year. Instead, a strategic long-range plan focuses on a powerful movement toward the achievement of strategic priorities—with an openness to the possibility that God will call that congregation to new priorities of mission that are not as yet discerned.

Two Advantages

There are two advantages to this approach to strategic long-range planning. The first advantage is that it takes seriously the integrity and individuality of each church and each community. The purpose of this approach to strategic long-range planning is to develop a creative match of nine central characteristics that will enable a church to be effective and successful. No effort is made to suggest that it must be any certain nine of the twelve. No effort is made to suggest that it must be all twelve of the twelve.

Rather, this approach to strategic long-range planning affirms that churches will be effective and successful insofar as they claim, expand, and add nine of the twelve central characteristics in a way that takes seriously the indigenous character of their own church and their own community. Such an approach frees local churches from a compulsive search for perfection. It is precisely this search for perfection that sets churches up to fail and, thereby, lowers their sense of self-esteem. Too many pastors and too many congregations are addicted to a compulsiveness that destroys the very confidence and competence that God seeks to share with the congregation.

The second advantage of this approach is that it is neither absolute nor universal. One of the mistakes that some denominational leaders make is to advocate that a given approach should be used in virtually every congregation across the land. Denominational offices frequently promote a particular approach to mission as *the* approach that should be universally adopted in order for churches to be effective and successful. This approach suggests, rather, that there are a minimum of absolutes and universals that advance the mission of a local congregation. To be sure, all effective, successful congregations have well in place at least nine of the twelve characteristics, but a different nine. This approach to planning fights the temptation in many denominational offices to advocate that a given gimmick will "do wonders" to advance the life and mission of any congregation. Indeed, in this country, it seems that local churches gravitate to gimmicks and fads as though these would cure their ills.

This approach to strategic long-range planning is hard work. It requires tough decisions related to the very foundations of a congregation. It invites a competency and courage in long-range planning that is rare. It would be difficult to find persons with these particular skills even in denominational offices, although there is a wide array of resource persons who do give effective leadership in the national offices of many denominations. Rather, this approach to long-range planning focuses on foundational chacteristics in a thoughtful and analytical way. The decisive directions that advance the mission of congregations are to be based on these foundational characteristics, not on gimmicks and gadgets that finally give way in the face of the tough issues of mission in our time.

Wisdom, Judgment, and Vision

To some extent, it is easy to develop a realistic assessment of a congregation's present standing and stature. Further, it is comparatively easy to think through the primary direction of that local church's future. It is also reasonably easy to study and assess which of the central strengths are currently well in place in a specific local congregation. To be sure, to do these things requires genuine honesty and mature integrity, but the steps are comparatively straightforward in the development of a strategic long-range plan.

The hardest part of strategic long-range planning is to put well in place a thoughtful plan that (1) takes seriously as many of the variables as possible, (2) considers which strategic priorities it makes sense to advance, (3) constructs these strategic priorities in the light of the four basic principles of strategic long-range planning, and (4) develops a strategic long-range plan that enables a congregation to be increasingly in mission in competent, compassionate, and courageous ways.

Long-range planning is finally an art—an art that entails wisdom, judgment, and vision. Wisdom, judgment, and vision can be learned, but they cannot be taught. To some extent, it may be possible to teach the rudiments, but to a large extent these qualities are gained through experience.

The quality and character of a given strategic long-range plan will be shaped by (1) the extent to which those who develop that plan have taken seriously the materials that have been shared in this book, and (2) the extent to which they have wisdom, judgment, and vision gained from their life experiences. The art of long-range planning is complex. The simplistic approaches that have been used in previous years have not reflected the maturity that strategic long-range planning must have. This maturity is developed through experience: The more consistently and regularly the leaders of a congregation engage in strategic long-range planning, the more they will gain the experience and maturity that enables them to do long-range planning with wisdom, judgment, and vision.

Strategic long-range planning will develop increasingly effective and successful congregations. Its driving direction is mission. It is my compelling conviction that God calls His churches to be effective and successful in mission. Strategic long-range planning helps the congregation to overcome its preoccupation with its own problems and to focus on those strengths that are well in place, those that can be intentionally expanded, and those that can be added. These strengths are not for their own sake but for the sake of mission.

In Revelation 21:5, these words are found: "And He who sat upon the throne said, 'Behold, I make all things new.'" God calls His local churches to the newness of mission. God goes before His people and invites them to that future that He has both promised and prepared. Strategic long-range planning is one resource that helps local congregations to discover what God is calling them to do in mission in the years to come.